My Blackberry Seed Legacy
"Unfinished Conversations with My Father"

By Alphonso Braggs, MBA

Foreword by Earl S. Braggs

Copyright © 2021 by Alphonso Braggs. All rights reserved. No part of this book may be reproduced or transmitted in any form or by any means, electronic or mechanical, including photocopying, recording or by any information storage and retrieval system, without written permission from the author, except for the inclusion of brief quotations in a review.

ISBN: 978-0-578-82987-6

Library of Congress Control Number: 2020920105

For questions or inquiries, contact the author: abraggs357@gmail.com

Published in Honolulu, Hawaii, United States of America
First Edition, 2021

Warning—Disclaimer: This book is written with the expressed intent to communicate the author's personal thoughts regarding conversations he would have with his father. It is not intended to be a reference for technical, historical, legal, or other professional benefit other than its social benefit. On subject matters where technical, historical, legal, or other professional assistance is required, the reader should consult with an authorized provider of desired services. The author shall have neither liability nor responsibility to any person or entity with respect to any loss or damage caused, or alleged to have been caused, directly or indirectly, by the information contained in this book. If you do not wish to be bound by the above, you may return this book to the publisher for a full refund.

Table of Contents

Table of Contents	*v*
Acknowledgments, Dedication, and Epigraph	*vi*
Foreword	*vii*
Prologue	*ix*
1. The Origin of the Blackberry Patch	*1*
2. The Bragg Seed	*9*
3. A Woman Named Ruth	*21*
4. A Foundation of Faith and Fortitude	*27*
5. Sustained by Grace	*37*
6. Singing Zion's Song	*45*
7. The Captivating Love of the Blackberry Nectar	*51*
8. Growing Friendship Vines	*59*
9. A Good Man Made Better	*69*
10. There Goes an Alpha Man	*75*
Epilogue - - We Need to Leave a Legacy	*81*
About the Author	*85*
References and Sources	*86*
Photos	*89*

Acknowledgments

I would not be where I am today had it not been for the Divine nurturing, astute mentoring, and fervent prayers and supplications of Mrs. Margaret M. Baham, Presiding Elder E. S. Hassell, Mrs. Fannie D. Holmes, Rev. Robert W. Johnson, Mrs. Posey W. Johnson, Dr. J.F.K. McCormick, Mrs. Connie B. Odell, Mr. E. L. Pettiford, Rev. Donald W.H.E. Ruffin, Bishop Herbert B. Shaw, Mrs. Margaret Simmons, Mrs. Bertha Todd, Rev. Barbara Vaughan, Rev. John E. Watts, Mrs. Geneva Watts, and Mrs. Margaret S. Williams. I also want to thank my friends, mentors, and mentees for giving me purpose and allowing me to share Grandma Ruth's love and dedication, especially Khyri Baker, Victor Blair, Fred Clark, Bruce James, Marsha Johnson, Norman Lloyd, James Nunnelly, and Josue Reyes.

Dedication

To
The Blackberry Seed Caretaker, Ruth E. Spicer Bragg

The Originator of my Blackberry Seed, Edward Earl Bragg

The Blackberry Seeds that grew in my garden patch
Andrew, Andre, Angelica, Allyson, Brandy, Francklyn, Monica, and Ryan

The Bearers of Blackberry Seeds including Cathy Ann Ramassar and Patricia Ann Collins

The Blackberry Seed project manager, Earl S. Braggs

Epigraph

"Give peace a chance and in the meantime—love!"

Foreword

By Earl S. Braggs

The Beautiful Silence of Love

According to the Russian poet Anna Akhmatova, "You wish that life could be put back together where it has been torn apart, but there is no such glue." The novelist James Baldwin tells us that, "The world is held together by the love of a few people, a very few people." After many years of falling in and out, I know now. Love by any definition is the best that we can do. This is a salute to my brother, Alphonso Braggs—a salute for saluting our grandmother, Ruth E. Bragg. Love is the best we can do. Grandmamma Ruth knew this and lived beyond this. Learned from birth or learned as she went along, I don't know. I suppose it matters not when "how love comes to be" is configured by whatever Cupid you believe in, then factored back into "the impact it had upon each of us," the beautifully spoken, yet unspoken silence of love. My earliest memory is the sound of noise, a steel garbage can being blown down the city streets of Wilmington, North Carolina by the terrible, yet wonderfully beautiful grace of gale forces, a hurricane the people called Hazel. Hazel-eyed pretty in ways most would call unaccountable routes, Hazel laid fear upon Cape Fear, but we were not afraid. We were storm-water people. That was a year or two before Grandmamma Ruth took me to live with her in the soul and heart of another kind of storm. Hampstead, North Carolina was a small fishing village then, whereupon the southern edge in a one-room shack, Grandmamma and I lived at the very bottom of love. I loved the George Washington live oak tree, branches of which we lived beneath. I loved Highway 17, the last highway on the east coast of our world. Only General George Washington and the Revolutionary War Monument separated our one-room shack from the two directions of traffic patterns, Highway 17. I loved the Gypsies who stopped daily to rest-stop beneath the shade of my George Washington oak tree. Close enough to the sea to see the salt in the air, I loved my saltwater life there. And there Grandmamma Ruth and I lived until I moved to the city to start 1st grade.

City life was not as kind as country life. After I'd lived three years with Mom and Dad and my brothers, Grandmamma claimed me again. This time the twins Alphonso and Alonzo, Anthony Lee, Tyrone, Grandmamma, and me became a family. This time we lived in a larger shack at the village center on the edge of a field where soil was too poor to grow anything but weeds and briars. We lived a happy-sad life, and as some say, I would not trade it for the world. Dirt poor, in need of everything but love, we lived, five black boys in an all-white town. Simon and Naomi, the only other black people living in Hampstead, helped, as much as they could, show us the way. Seaweed children we were. Wood-burning stove, hole in the kitchen floor, newspaper-insulated walls, commercials on every page, dirt front yard, no sign of a car in a two-rut-road driveway, and snakes on the front porch in the summer are just some of the images of a hard but happy-sad life. Another image is that of roasted oysters in November and shrimp and clams and flounders and brim and croakers and fried spots and Virginia mullets and cornbread and collard greens, a photograph of what raised each of us strong. We lived off the land just as much as we lived in the sea. Grandmamma taught us all to love the smell of salt in saltwater life.

Life torn apart, never at the seams, Grandmamma knew there was no such glue. She used tape. With seams tied together with the strong threads of a grandmother's love, my brother Alphonso takes what was given and not given and pieces together **My Blackberry Seed Legacy**. With attention to the nuances of a mostly unwritten family history, he climbs cliffs never scaled. He dreams then draws lines, long erased. History is revealed, and in the brilliance and shadows thereof, love. I love this book as it journeys its way from "our town," Browntown, to other towns—towns that still record our family's footprints in the mud, dirt, and sands of time. "Let it not be forgotten" is the theme here, and the "Honor" here is the truth and the light of remembering. As a poet, I say, "You must lock yourself around the rhythm of a place," and in Alphonso's case, a face, and many faces. Alphonso locked himself around the nectar of a blackberry seed that happens to be ours. "Ours" means everybody below, above, and right on the line. Yet specifically "ours" is the family, the overturning, the dissecting, the honoring of each part of a history of triangles, straight lines, circles, and squares. Alphonso dares each of us to not only read the words and view the intent of each photograph, but to see and hear and feel and listen to and touch that which is between, below, and above it all, love, the beautiful silence of.

Prologue

I decided to take time and put pen to paper on things I wanted to or should have discussed with my father. The following chapters tell of my journey balancing life without my father. It has not been an easy journey, and by some of my choices, I made the rough pathways more difficult to travel.

Yet, I am grateful for my humble beginnings because they continue to keep me grounded, and the immoveable spiritual bond with a woman named Ruth allows me to stay focused on my Heavenly Father's purpose. These unfinished conversations address my blackberry seed legacy in three primary areas: foundation, friendship, and fraternity.

Foundation addresses three core elements of Alphonso the man: my faith, family, and stewardship. I discuss the joy in knowing that my faith has sustained me during difficult times, the empowerment that comes from singing the songs of Zion, the beauty of genuinely loving others, and the unmerited blessings of having friends. Foundation celebrates the family, elders, mentors, and pillars of my community.

I address how this foundation helped me become a mature and properly developed adult. I also share the pride I gained from learning about my biological ancestors. I am humbled by a better understanding of their struggles, faithful commitments, and significant sacrifices. Of course, I had to dedicate a special section to one of my foundation pillars, my paternal grandmother, Ruth Bragg; without her, I know I would not be the man I am today.

Stewardship addresses how I am committed to being a responsible conservator of my rich heritage as a man, a citizen, and cultural and ethnic representative. Specifically, I address leaving a legacy that demonstrates my duty to be a good steward of my name, heritage, and community. It addresses how

I must be a dutiful citizen to God, my neighbor, and self. It speaks about my lifelong commitment to pay it forward.

It is an honest reflection of maturing wisdom. When I break it down, it speaks about how my foundation gave me what I needed to stand upright as a man, father, brother, and leader while bringing honor and value to the legacy of our blackberry seed. The chapters of this book address topics that my children should be discussing with their children and grandchildren. I have taken the liberty of sharing areas of engagement I know would make my father proud. The two primary persons to whom this book is dedicated have now gone on to eternal rest.

Sharing in this manner I believe will benefit my children and grandchildren. They will never know firsthand the love, commitment, and soul-stirring influence Ruth Bragg could impose. It is difficult to really explain without getting emotional about just how much I owe for her unconditional love and commitment to my well-being.

I believe one of the major requirements my father would insist is that this book gives due deference to his beloved mother. He knew that she was a person of substantial faith and that she taught us to be likewise. At times, my children, friends, and other family members find it ironic that I am primarily governed by an unrelenting desire to extend a portion of her legacy in my daily encounters.

I want them to know that the love of the blackberry seed resonates in us all. I want them to know that because they carry this special blackberry seed forward, they also have the burden of ensuring future generations never let go of its special nectar. I would be remiss if I failed to validate and document her legacy and contributions. The least that I can do is offer future generations, through a more permanent means, a few of her philosophies. Each day I pray that my children will never forget that I love them and want them to have a better life than I, my father, or his father.

In my most private moments, it affirms the deep longing I have for a loving and committed relationship with my children despite the fear of getting too close—not knowing when it will be my time to return to the earth whence, I came. Quite honestly, I never want them to experience my childhood ordeals, especially feeling incomplete based on family construct.

I think it is important for future generations to understand the symbolic connection of the severed blackberry vine and the reason. Let me use the example of the distinct similarity between a father and a farmer. There are some things about farming that only a farmer can teach. Likewise, there are many things about being a parent that only a parent can teach. Life teaches us that you don't have to own the farm to farm the crop and yield a bountiful harvest.

The farmer ensures a good harvest because he shows others the value of cultivating the land so that it yields a bounty that gives back to the farm, farmer, family, and community. Included is the more noble purpose that the overflow is shared among those in need. Perhaps that rationalization is the reason for my strong desire for paternal relationships.

Unless you have walked in my shoes or traveled down my paths, you cannot begin to imagine the impact losing my dad had on my life at such an early age. Grandma Ruth taught us that no matter how painful the void, God is able to fill it if we place our trust in Him. It also explains why I am so emotionally torn when I discern the absence of paternal engagement in others.

I am personally pained by the reality of such cases and feel that no person should have to go without that which God has planted in a father's heart. Grandma Ruth was a tremendous woman. I could not tell my story without telling how her tender gardening of the blackberry patch has yielded a bountiful harvest. I know she is proud. I thank her for teaching me to respect this proud legacy. Growing up in the South, we were taught the more purposeful way to live, and Grandma ensured it was part of our daily routine.

I feel it is important for my seed to learn to cultivate society so that future generations will produce healthy seeds of purpose. The legacy was unfurled on the day I faced my fears, stepped out on faith, and accepted that it was time for Alphonso to sow his own blackberry seed and let a new vine in this **blackberry patch**. Looking back, it seemed like the men in our family had quite a few women and children. This made me nervous about becoming a dad. In the end, I found it to be one of the greatest blessings on earth.

I'm sure Dad and my grandparents would be proud and how, with the help of God, I have managed to love and provide for them as their father. Now, they are fathers and proudly carry the rich legacy of our blackberry seed forward. ***"It was painful when you died, and I was not happy that I did not get to see you before you passed."***

For many years while the kids were growing up, I worried about how long I would live. I felt like Dad, Grandpa Henry, and Uncle Ernest died far too young. With this in mind, health is very important to me. Thus, these conversations are also intended to help me, my children, and their children have some closure. My dedication to this blackberry seed legacy represents a commitment to my ancestors.

In a small way, I am working to honor those who made it possible for my present station in life. I wish to document through written word how the people who have had the greatest personal influence on my life made a good man better. This is due to my belief that as humans, we tend to forget more as we grow older.

Additionally, I like to share good thoughts and inspirational words of wisdom because they really do help. So, these are what some of the conversations with my father would entail. I know that he and Grandma Ruth are looking down from Heaven with a huge smile of affirmation. Don't get me wrong. This does not substitute for the wonderful sharing I have with my children and grandchildren. I just want to put it down for them to have permanently.

Finally, it's impossible to discuss our family's journey without acknowledging our Christian upbringing. After all, it has been our rudder in rough seas and a guiding light along dangerous pathways. Given that golden chance of a few minutes with Dad, I think he would emphasize the importance of building healthy relationships based on the values of family, friends, and faith. I can only pray that I get it right as I share with my children and grandchildren my blackberry seed legacy.

"Origin of the Blackberry Patch"

I know I am of a strong blackberry vine. I am so grateful that I was able to trace the sweet nectar of this blackberry vine back to the late 1700s. As I reflected on the symbolism of the blackberry seed in the technical sense, I learned that there are several varieties. I am particularly fond of the **"Thornless Black Satin"** specimen. Much like my North American ancestors, it originated in the Southeast United States and is often described as a large, firm, and glossy blackberry. Yes, it is an attractive specimen and highly sought after to produce high-quality jams and jellies or to simply savor its sweetness fresh off the vine.

I am the genealogical product of slaves, slave owners, and those whom American archives verify were displaced by both, the Native Americans. In particular, my ancestral roots are of the Native American Cherokee Tribe. A lot of theory has been made about the source of our last name. The most common analogy is that the slaves took on the last name of their owners. Thus, we presume that we were at one time owned by the Bragg family in North Carolina.

History teaches that, like most things in nature, little boys eventually transition into young men and are subsequently given the opportunity to sow new seeds. Regardless of the path this vine takes, I see strong blackberry seeds blessed of the lush morning dew and ready for harvest. The blackberry seed—much like the human seed—requires unique conditions for growth and maximum development. These conditions ensure that the seed, when properly planted and well nourished, fulfills the maker's purpose and enhances the harvester's value. Research further shows that both the blackberry seed and my African ancestors made their way to America across the great Atlantic, and over time added to its rich legacy by yielding their presence and production to that of the Creator's purpose.

I am one of those statistical kids who grew up without a father in the home. My vine was further stressed because my parents were separated shortly after I was born, and I did not live in my parents' household for nine of my first ten years. Depending on the family's dysfunction, a kid may experience significant trauma, as most are not prepared to deal with the unplanned departure from the home and/or the sudden death of a parent. Stress, trauma, and dysfunction will usually have an adverse impact on the season's harvest. Although God in His infinite wisdom saw fit to cut my father from our family's vine at an early age, He saw to it that none of the season's harvests sustained permanent damage. ***"Dad, I am very proud of the strong wine that continues to flow from harvesting this blackberry seed."***

Personally, I feel like life cheated me twice. One of my biggest fears I held on to for the longest is not living as long as my father and leaving my young children fatherless. I was afraid my children would carry the same pain I endured. I still worry about them even though now they are grown with children. I worry if they have come to a place in their lives to know that God will comfort them in their deepest hours of sorrow. I feel strongly that the absence of my father cemented the construct and conditions of my relationships. These emotions generate questions that only my father and God can answer. They are all part of an unfinished conversation I regularly internalize having with my father.

"Dad, my deepest desire is to just talk to you about things fathers and sons should discuss." I cannot put into words how badly I want to hear his thoughts on world events or process his advice as a second opinion. I am torn that I shall never hear his admonishment or parental affirmation. I will forever live with the unanswered question regarding making him proud of my accomplishments. There are so many things I face each day that I would like to discuss with him. I never desired to ask him the why this or why that. I just wanted to be able to talk to him and enjoy the simple comfort in knowing he is there should I need to call. There is a part of me that longs to hear his feedback on how well I tended the blackberry vine over the years and whether he felt I rendered a reasonable harvest.

I am not sure if I told him that I loved him the last time I saw him. Quite frankly, I don't recall much about our last departure. All I know is that I saw this statue of a man fade into the distance. I will forever hold this memory near and dear to my heart. As I age and memories fade, these treasured memories of the times we spent are crystalized as though they were yesterday. The times were few, but they are indelible and among life's most celebrated. His last visit did not have such a profound meaning at the time, because I always had a reasonable expectation that fate would grant me a future visit, a memorable fellowship, a positive and enriching engagement with the man whose blackberry seed I was now blessed to sprout future vines. Would we be down at the fish house on the Cape Fear River where he had worked?

Would it be at the café where we sat in the kitchen enjoying hot dogs? Would it be at Grandma Ruth's house for one of his visits? Perhaps it would be one of my trips to town with a visit to his house on Orange Street. Oh, how I loved playing on the stoop and running up and down the steps at his house. Sadly, I took for granted that my vine could be cut off so abruptly. I took for granted that I would have to learn about letting this blackberry vine on my own. Likewise, I don't recall telling him that I was proud of him, the man. Moreover, I don't think it was an important matter for me at that age.

What I understood was that in his brief life, he earned a reputation for drinking, chasing women, and a few other unspeakables. I can't say that he was the best example of a father, husband, or friend. This may all be true; however, for me, those things were secondary. ***"Dad, all that matters to me is that you are my dad and that's good enough for me to love you and want you in my life."*** I was taught that with the power of God's love, all other issues could be resolved. I never thought that there were other conditions or requirements for a kid to want and love his or her parent. That is the way that Grandma Ruth raised us to love and respect. This is the message I pass on each day to young couples and pray future generations will understand.

I loved my dad and wanted him in my life. I am proud that I am the fruit of my father's loins. Whatever and wherever the seed may have fallen short, I now have the burden of making the harvest plenty and the fruit good. It's an inseparable pride and love. Perhaps my reasons for feeling so strongly about my dad are based on our life circumstances and the emotions they created. They are the direct cause of my heart's conviction and the ones I will take to my grave. They are pure for me because they are genuine and even respectful. The way I feel about my dad speaks volumes about how I engage relationships. Family and friends will confirm that I rarely move away from a relationship unless it is for health reasons. I must maintain a healthy vine, or I cannot produce healthy fruit at harvest time. While I have a high tolerance for many things, most people familiar with me will tell you that once the vine is cut, it's difficult to splice back together again. I believe strongly in forgiveness, and then I work on peaceful living. Forgiveness is necessary, and love must be paramount for a healthy relationship to exist.

I know that anything that blocks love coming or going is not healthy and has to be removed. The key to it all is a thing called love, and not a form of love or pretense or conditional situation. At this stage of my life, I have resolved that pure love removes all volatile situations or obstructions to a healthy relationship. I also believe that love is worth fighting for in a loving manner. My greatest comfort in life comes from being taught at an early age to respect and appreciate that I am my father's seed. It was the woman who nourished his father's seed who taught us that regardless of the situation, God would see us through. Consequently, I and my seed have been able to navigate troubled waters as children and adults. I attribute my daily survival to the unconditional love and commitment of Grandma Ruth and her empowering example of faith in God.

Like the farmer's devoted care toward his freshly planted seed, God used Ruth Bragg to ensure that this little kid received a sustainable portion of proper nourishment and development. As in childhood, adult life presented me with substantial events for which had I not been duly prepared and properly positioned, and there would have been less than desired outcomes. Being able to draw on the strength and love imbued by Ruth Bragg, I was able to endure and push on to see another bountiful harvest season come to pass. Although my father's days on this earth were cut short, I feel there are a lot of things that he would have liked to make sure I knew and passed on to my children and grandchildren. I don't think he would have let me forget about my foundation. I want to think that he believed his greatest achievement was having his kids' lives significantly influenced by his mother. That to me makes him a winner. He understood what we needed to survive, and he did not try to impede it from happening. I could be wrong.

However, because the stars aligned in my favor, psychologically, I believe I am right. I also believe it gave him immeasurable peace as a parent struggling with the socio-economic dynamics of life. Honestly, I believe that not enough research is done to determine how men really feel about being separated from their kids. ***"Dad, how did you feel?"***

I think that he would have insisted that his seed knew and deeply respected our rich cultural heritage and pushed for us to achieve. I don't think that he took comfort or showed pride for his shortcomings but privately gave thanks to God that perhaps better days lay ahead for his kids than what he experienced. All too often we think that men, especially black and brown men, are content with the absence when the opposite is the reality. Perhaps macho pride, shame, and other factors prevented us from coming forward with our true feelings. However, it warrants consideration. I am certain that the general conclusion is far from the truth.

The research and oral history conducted in the writing of this book has been more than an enlightening experience. It has been a most amazing look at American history and certainly not the one I received in the classroom during parochial school. The revelations discovered in this research project have definitely generated new research projects for me and my family. I am convinced more now than ever that I owe it to future generations to try to answer the questions my ancestors did not about who we are and where we came from. I believe that their primary reason for not passing on as much ancestral history as possible was due to their individual circumstances.

Research and interviews of family members revealed that many members of my family were unable to read and write, which does not mean that they did not intend to share their story. Our basic knowledge of our African history teaches us that so many of our legacies were passed down by spoken word from one generation to another. I was blessed to learn that some of our recent history was preserved in family bibles and other journal forms by folks in the community able to read and write. I am grateful for the information they preserved and did pass on, and I will endeavor to give it a more permanent means to transition the legacy of this blackberry seed to future generations. The research of this book also revealed a lot to me about the men who carry the name Bragg. These blackberry seeds were plentiful, and they sprouted many blackberry patches. These men were blessed with strong and devoted God-fearing women who supported their offspring on this journey called life, and in turn the Bragg blackberry seed continues to yield a bountiful harvest.

My elders had a unique way of teaching the principles of appropriate living. It seemed they were always talking in adult riddles. Reflecting back, I think they meant for us to hear them but not understand them. Now that I am an adult and can recall their conversations, they have profound meanings. Actually, I would say they are more than profound. They are priceless principles to guide us through life. They literally become effective tools for mentoring, parenting, and teaching life skills. I take pride in using them to help today's young adults cope with life's challenges. Therefore,

I am committed to passing on to my children and grandchildren information that will help them better understand the culture of our ancestors. This will allow them to make and pass on a more informed understanding as to why a lot of our ancestors did not put pen to paper.

The available technical archives of the late 1800s and early 1900s helped me to paint a mental picture of what life was like living in the typical Bragg's household. I can visualize my ancestors living and working on spacious farmlands throughout rural North Carolina. I can only surmise that those of the recent centuries were sharecropping on the same land their ancestors toiled in the heat of the day as slaves. I see the women as housekeepers and servants. It also appears that the men did not get into the white-collar jobs until after the first quarter of the 20th century. The families moved around, and the only reasons I could surmise were jobs and family situations. Research shows that most of the family migrated primarily along U.S. Highway 17 from the Wilmington, North Carolina Coast through New Hanover, Pender, Onslow, and Craven Counties. Along the way they sowed many blackberry patches.

Reflecting back on my elders' conversations growing up, I always heard them speak about how easy it was for a man to make a baby. Of course, it was quickly followed by comments recognizing the men who did their part to help raise their kids. I think they were planting seeds of responsibility to those of us listening that should we endeavor to sow seeds, we must be responsible. Given the behaviors they knew of our fathers' fathers, they wanted to make sure we also understood the associated responsibility and commitment the village expected from a Bragg father. Symbolically, the elders also helped us learn the value of the thorns in the blackberry briar patch and the role they played in defending the unripened berries from premature picking. In retrospect, they were invoking the intellectual depth and symbolic collective duty of the African proverb: "it takes a village." ***"Dad, do you remember these talks as a kid?"***

They were reminding us of its broader meaning for future generations of blackberry seeds. They taught us lessons on valuing our produce and ensuring it stayed on the vine until harvest time. I want my children and grandchildren to know these profound lessons of survival from our ancestors and how they promote pride in our heritage. I also want to proclaim how proud I am to carry the Bragg name forward. ***"Dad, where did the "s" come from?"*** This book research has caused me to seriously consider removing the letter "s" from my last name. *Pride starts somewhere*. For me, it began with my people, the bloodline of the blackberry seed—the faces I grew up with as a child. It expanded with the knowledge and understanding of their struggles and sacrifices. How could I accept this and be anything less than a proud black man?

Additionally, it reinforced my determination to live with an independent mind and free will. I shall never take for granted the rights and freedoms I have as a citizen, not by any means. I know it is the result of many black men and women suffering before me, and that knowledge gives me immense culture and heritage pride. Thus, if you witness a certain modulation in tone or hypnotic acclaim when I proclaim the legacy and richness of my blackberry seed, you will know why. Whether it's the Biblical accounts of brave souls taking a stand for God and family or the piercing accounts of the legacy and beauty of Native Americans, I realize that our blackberry patches are not that far removed. We are of the same indigenous root. This is why I believe that my ancestors held on to the belief that although they came not to die for future generations, they were committed to do so if necessary because they had a vision of what I could become. I must tell our story to my children and love them so they will tell their children the story of these great bearers of strong blackberries.

The Blackberry Seed Name
"Bragg" or "Braggs"

You got it from your father; It was all he had to give

So, it's yours to use and cherish;

For as long as you may live.

If you lose the watch, he gave you;

It can always be replaced.

But a black mark on your name son;

Can never be erased.

It was clean the day you took it;

And a worthy name to bear.

When he got it from his father;

There was no dishonor there.

So make sure you guard it wisely;

After all is said and done.

You'll be glad the name is spotless,

When you give it to your son.

Author unknown

"The Bragg Seed"

This research and unfinished conversations are an endeavor that will continue by me and future fathers' generations as we give honor to the legacy of our blackberry seed. The earliest known and documented information available on Bragg's blackberry seed vine was used to establish the first generation. While it is not the beginning, it is a great starting point to celebrate our rich legacy. Here is a mapping of strong blackberry seeds from the Bragg's blackberry patches.

First (Alpha) Bragg Generation - *Great-Great-Great-Grandfather (Unknown) Bragg*

My great-great-great-grandfather was born in North Carolina according to the 1880 U.S. Census records. While he and his wife's names are unknown to me at this time, the records show that they were both born in North Carolina. The distinction of "Unknown" Bragg designation as the first generation is only in the context of known information and my ability to legally validate the generation from credentialed sources. It is obvious that many ancestors came before them, but we are unable to locate and document them at this time.

1st Bragg Generation Child No. (?), Parents: Unknown:

Alfred Bragg, my great-great-grandfather, was born in April 1825 in North Carolina.

Given the information available from U.S. Census records of births, locations, and names, I accept the highest probability that my great-great-grandfather was not an only child. However, because I could not definitively determine dates of birth, exact location, and accurate names proving the manner of relationship, some relatives are not shown in this section. A review of the census data for Negro males living in North Carolina during this period of his life and their primary occupations leads me to conclude that he worked on a farm. This was also the main occupation listed in census records for other family members during this period. I am also inclined to believe that he lived in the same vicinity of Eastern North Carolina. This is based on census records of other Bragg family members who are not immediate descendants of him but obviously related to him.

Second Bragg Generation - *Great-Great-Grandfather Alfred Bragg*

Born in North Carolina, April 1825—Given that the official census reports that Alfred Bragg was not the first of my vine, I will list him as leading the second blackberry patch in this village. According to the 1880 U.S. Census Report, my **great-great-grandfather** was named ***Alfred Bragg***, and he lived in the Grant Township of Pender County, North Carolina. The census enumerator recorded his birth date as April 1825 and his occupation as a turpentine hand. He was listed as the head of his household along with his wife, my **great-great-grandmother Mary (Butler) Edwards**, a housekeeper. She was born June 1853 in Wadesboro, North Carolina. They were married in 1870. Some sources list her father as Dave Edwards. According to the 1900 U.S. Census Report, he had been married for 30 years. This would have put him at the age of 45, and his bride would have been approximately 17 years old when they married. Based on the age of my great-great-grandfather Alfred at the time he married my great-great-grandmother Mary, I suspect that he had other children from a previous marriage or marriages. As a child I was told this was the case. The census data from the 1900 report did not indicate the number of marriages per individual. However, the 1910 census reported the number of marriages by listing the status as "M1" in contrast with "M" as shown on the 1900 U.S. Census Report.

Several of these ancestral records of our ancestors have discrepancies and omissions regarding dates of birth and ages at times the records were being recorded. I was taken aback by the discovery of differences in the information that was provided to the various government agencies. For example, information provided to the census taker differs significantly in some cases from the information provided to the Social Security Administration or the Draft Registration Agents. Many of the differences show the individuals being reported as younger at the time of death. However, some errors about a person's age on the census reports are obvious math miscalculations. I interviewed family members regarding disparities in reporting to government officials. Several of my elders informed me that differences in ages were due to protect eligibility of benefits such as insurance, keeping family matters private, and conditions of employment. From a technical research point of view, I think it is important to share that many of the records show changes in locality when in fact the property was in the same location. I found a book that will help readers and future generations better understand these occurrences. While conducting research, I came across a publication entitled, *THE CLARENDON COURIER—Journal of The Old New Hanover Genealogical Society.* The publication addresses the expansion of people and counties in Eastern North Carolina. This article gives some perspective on the changes that took place throughout the states as populations changed and expansions took place. Volume 15, Number 1, 2003, of the journal reported that *"**Pender County was a part of New Hanover until 1875, when it was partitioned to form a separate county. In 1869, the area which was to become Pender County had the following townships: Grant, Holden, Lincoln, Caswell, Columbia, Franklin, Union, and Holly. By 1880, the township names of Franklin, Grant, Holden, and Lincoln were changed, and the boundaries were redrawn. The current townships are: Canetuck, Caswell, Grady, Long Creek, Rocky Point, Topsail, Holly, Burgaw, Columbia, and Union.**"*

The 1900 and 1910 U.S. Census Reports show our family roots in the Stump Sound Township, Onslow County, North Carolina, while the 1880 U.S. Census Report shows our family living in Grant Township, Pender County, North Carolina. Further research shows the family living in New Hanover County. It wasn't so much as the family had moved but also that the county lines and townships were changing. The following paragraphs provide basic information on the family roots. I covered the basic information on the siblings of my direct line. Alfred and Mary had several children together and lived throughout these Southeast counties in various townships. I will use the system of listing each generation with the parents and the number of siblings connected to that line of Bragg blackberry seed.

2nd Bragg Generation Child No. 1, Parents: Alfred and Mary:

William Henry Bragg, my great-grandfather, was born on July 20, 1878, in North Carolina. The 1880 Census report lists his birth at the time of the census as four years old. He is reported in subsequent census reports and other documents as Henry, without the name William. He is the eldest child.

2nd Bragg Generation Child No. 2, Parents: Alfred and Mary:

Charles (Charley) Bragg was born in Pender County, North Carolina in March 1880. He was married to Susan (born March 1881). The 1880 Census report lists his birth at the time of the census as three years old. This uncle is of particular interest to me because he is the one I heard a lot of stories about during my childhood. Additionally, I was raised around several of his children. Uncle Charles and Aunt Susan had seven children. Calvin Bragg was born in 1903. Joseph Bragg was born in October 1905. Edward Bragg was born in 1907. Mary Bragg was born in 1908. Alfred and Albert Bragg were born in March 1910. Cousin Charley's second wife was Annie. She was born in 1877. Their son Jimmie was born in 1920. Their daughter Lucy was born in 1924. Cousins Alfred and Albert were twins. Until my identical twin brother Alonzo and I were born in 1960, no Bragg twins had been born into our family for fifty years. This made us special and valued in the family. It is also interesting to note that Grandma Ruth's sister Evalene married one of the twins, making Cousin Alfred and me doubly related. It appears Uncle Charley lived nearby or next door to the family along with his wife Susan, based on the census enumerator's records. As a child I recall fondly wonderful visits with Cousin Lucy, Cousin Mary, and Cousin Joseph (affectionately referred to as Uncle Joe Bragg). Cousin Joseph was married to Miss Nora, and they were considered upper class among the family and neighbors.

Grandma Ruth became very close to the entire family, and Cousin Joseph played a monumental role in providing for Grandma Ruth during difficult times. I have fond memories of visits to Uncle Charley's children's homes and their visits to Grandma Ruth's. The research for this book helped me to discover the connection between folks who were identified as family and further explained why this bond was so strong. We also attended the same family church in Browntown. I cannot recall a time where they did not extend a helping hand to take care of my siblings and me. Uncle Charley died in Hampstead, North Carolina on January 17, 1935, at the age of 54, from heart problems. At the time of his death, he was living in the Topsail area and still married to his wife Annie. He was buried in Holly Ridge, North Carolina on January 20, 1935.

2nd Bragg Generation Child No. 3, Parents: Alfred and Mary:

Priscilla Bragg was born on March 30, 1889, in North Carolina. Her children and their approximate years of birth included Nellie, 1905; Edith, 1906; Linwood, 1908; Hilda, 1910; Roberta, 1914; and

Elnora, 1916. She was married to Tobe Sidberry. She died on October 27, 1971, in New Bern, Craven County, North Carolina.

2nd Bragg Generation Child No. 4, Parents: Alfred and Mary:

Mary A. Bragg was born on February 18, 1885, in North Carolina. She was married to Oscar Green (born approximately 1881), and their children were Ida Green (born 1904); Martha Green; Elizabeth Green (born approximately 1911); Louise (born approximately 1913); Arey Green (born approximately 1914); Andrew Green (born approximately 1908); William Thomas Green (born approximately 1919); Reuben Green; and Maude Green. She died of pneumonia on February 11, 1953, at the age of 57, in North Carolina.

2nd Bragg Generation Child No. 5, Parents: Alfred and Mary:

Lena Bragg was born in April 1886 in North Carolina.

2nd Bragg Generation Child No. 6, Parents: Alfred and Mary:

Laura Bragg was born February 1888 in North Carolina; I was able to find the death certificate for Aunt Laura showing she died of tuberculosis on November 9, 1915, in Middle Sound, Pender County. She was married to a H. Clay at the time of her death. She was buried in Middle Sound on November 10, 1915. She had suffered from tuberculosis for approximately six months before succumbing to the disease. The death certificate lists my great-grandfather as the father, which is more than likely because he was the oldest at the time of her death and the head of the family. The certificate lists an approximate year of birth as 1888. However, it states her age as 23 instead of 27.

2nd Bragg Generation Child No. 7, Parents: Alfred and Mary:

Donnings Bragg was born in May 1893. He is later identified in the census and other records as Don. His wife was Lila, and they had two children: Herman, born 1917, and John, born 1920. Lila is the sister of Sallie. Sallie is my great-grandfather William Henry Bragg's brother's third wife. He died on October 6, 1975, in Hampstead, North Carolina from heart problems at the reported age of 75.

The death certificate gives him a date of birth of January 2, 1900. There is a contradiction in his age on his death certificate and the census records. Both show he is the son of Alfred and Mary Bragg, but with different dates of birth. He was buried in the Community Cemetery on October 12, 1975.

2nd Bragg Generation Child No. 8, Parents: Alfred and Mary:

Lillie Bragg was born January 1895.

2nd Bragg Generation Child No. 9, Parents: Alfred and Mary:

Emma Bragg was born March 1896 in Holly Ridge, North Carolina. She is later shown on records as Mary Emma Sidbury. She died of tuberculosis in New Hanover County, North Carolina on March 26, 1937, at the age of 41. She was buried in Holly Ridge, North Carolina on March 28, 1937. Her primary occupation had been a domestic house worker for approximately 20 years of her adult life. She was a widow at the time of her death.

2nd Bragg Generation Child No. 10, Parents: Alfred and Mary:

Julia Bragg was born 1891. She was married to Christopher "Kit" Spicer. He preceded her in death in 1964. She passed on May 18, 1970, in Wilmington, North Carolina at the age of 79. Her funeral and burial were held at Enoch Chapel in Scotts Hill, Wilmington, North Carolina on May 24, 1970. Many of our family members knew and visited with her in Wilmington.

2nd Bragg Generation Child No. 11, Parents: Alfred and Mary:

The U.S. Census records reflect that Alfred and Mary were the parents of eleven children. However, I was not able to obtain exacting information on all the children. A Julia Harris passed on September 8, 1930, in New Bern Craven County, North Carolina. She was living at 16 Bloomfield Street and died at home according to her death certificate. She was born on June 10, 1882, in Craven County, North Carolina. Her death certificate lists Henry Bragg as the father and Mary Butler (maiden name) as the mother. The information was provided by Mary Bragg of New Bern, North Carolina. It reports an age of 48 and that she was single. She passed from cerebral problems and was buried in the Evergreen Cemetery on September 10, 1930.

Third Bragg Generation - *Great-Grandfather William Henry Bragg Sr.*

Born in North Carolina July 20, 1878—According to the 1900 U.S. Census Report, my great-grandfather William Henry Bragg Sr. lived in his father's home while growing up and after marrying his second wife. It appears that most of the siblings were still in the household by 1900 except his brother Charley. His date of birth on the 1900 U.S. Census Report is different from other government records. I was able to locate his draft registration card from 1918, and it gave the most specific date of birth recorded in government records while he was alive. The record shows he was farming for himself and living with his wife Della in Holly Ridge, Onslow County, North Carolina. He registered for the Draft at the age of 40 on September 12, 1918. Further research shows he had several wives. I was not able to obtain data on his **first marriage** other than the information provided to the enumerator for the 1910 U.S. Census Report that shows he was on his second marriage. His **second marriage** was to Della Batts in 1900. She was born in January 1881. This was her first marriage. This is also the first documented evidence of our family being classified as mixed or biracial as she is listed, and the children are listed as "mulatto" while my great-grandfather William Henry Bragg is listed as "Black." This is one of the most important affirmations since our family name came from our presumed white slave owners. It furthers validates the marriages of biracial women to black men during an era when those considered Black were prohibited from marrying outside of their race.

Little to no information is available on my great-grandmother. I was able to find information on an individual by the name of Della Batts; however, there is a discrepancy regarding her date of birth. She died on March 17, 1956, in Chinquapin, Duplin County, North Carolina from heart problems at the age of 75. She passed at the home of her brother Willie Batts. Her death certificate shows her date of birth as May 31, 1880; the 1900 U.S. Census Report shows a January 1881 date of birth. She was buried in the Batts Cemetery in Chinquapin, Duplin County, North Carolina on March 18, 1956. Her death certificate lists her race as white. This is an important factor to consider in my ancestral research and warrants further study. My great-grandfather's death certificate shows he died on November 7, 1952 at the age of 74 in New Bern, Craven County, North Carolina. He died at his residence on 1014 North Street, New Bern, North Carolina, and his death information was reported by my grandfather Henry Bragg. He died of heart problems. He was buried in the Evergreen Cemetery in New Bern, North Carolina on November 9, 1952. His death certificate affirms his parents as Alfred and Mary Bragg and shows he was separated from his wife at the time of death. My grandfather, his namesake, did not live much longer after his dad's death. He also succumbed to heart problems. Research on the cause of death of direct family members indicates a high percentage of deaths attributed to heart-related problems. My great-grandfather William Henry Bragg Sr. and Della's union produced six children, of which three survived according to the census reporting data from 1910. The three surviving children included my paternal grandfather, **William Henry Bragg Jr**. It is reasonable to presume that the three children were born sometime between 1897 when my Uncle Herbert was born and 1906 when my Aunt Bessie was born. It should also be noted that the 1900 U.S. Census Report has Great-Grandmother Della listed as the daughter and Uncle Herbert listed as the grandchild. His name is spelled differently—he is shown as Hulburt. I am listing the three unknown children consecutively for accountability purposes as I am not sure of their dates of birth. His **third marriage** was to Sallie Batts, born in September 1899. They were married on August 22, 1919.

3rd Bragg Generation Child No. 1, Parents: William Henry Sr. and Della:

Herbert Bragg, born April 1897.

3rd Bragg Generation Child No. 2, Parents: William Henry Sr. and Della:

Unknown Bragg—the U.S. Census records reflect that they were the parents of six children. However, I was not able to obtain information on all of them. Based on later census records providing information on the remaining three children, I presume this child was born before the others.

3rd Bragg Generation Child No. 3, Parents: William Henry Sr. and Della:

Unknown Bragg—the U.S. Census records reflect that they were the parents of six children. However, I was not able to obtain information on all of them. Based on later census records providing information on the remaining three children, I presume this child was born before the others.

3rd Bragg Generation Child No. 4, Parents: William Henry Sr. and Della:

Unknown Bragg—the U.S. Census records reflect that they were the parents of six children. However, I was not able to obtain information on all of them. Based on later census records providing information on the remaining three children, I presume this child was born before the others.

3rd Bragg Generation Child No. 5, Parents: William Henry Sr. and Della:

William Henry Bragg Jr.—my paternal grandfather was born on May 9, 1905, in Onslow County, North Carolina.

3rd Bragg Generation Child No. 6, Parents: William Henry Sr. and Della:

Bessie Bragg, born 1906. The only person I had the opportunity to meet from this union was my Aunt Bessie. I heard many stories of her when I was a kid. Her first marriage was to Ferris Henderson at the age of 16 on August 6, 1922. They had three children: Annie, born 1924; Geraldine, born 1925; and Ferris Jr., born 1929. On October 24, 1946 she married Amos Richard Leary at the age of 40. She died on June 11, 1988, at the age of 82.

3rd Bragg Generation Child No. 7, Parents: William Henry Sr. and Sallie:
Leroy Bragg, born 1920.

3rd Bragg Generation Child No. 8, Parents: William Henry Sr. and Sallie:

Miller Bragg, born May 26, 1922. He died in North Carolina in 2014. He was the last surviving child of my great-grandfather William Henry Bragg Sr.

3rd Bragg Generation Child No. 9, Parents: William Henry Sr. and Sallie:

Jessie Bragg, born June 8, 1926, was married to Mary L. Bragg. He died on April 1, 1956 in a motor vehicle accident on Highway 76 in the early morning in Wilmington, North Carolina at the age of 29. He is buried in the Batts Cemetery in Hampstead, North Carolina.

3rd Bragg Generation Child No. 10, Parents: William Henry Sr. and Sallie:

Lula Anne Bell Bragg, born June 11, 1927. She died in Wilmington, North Carolina on June 24, 1975. I was blessed to have many visits with my Aunt Lula and her family before she passed.

Fourth Bragg Generation - *Grandfather William Henry Bragg Jr.*

Born in North Carolina May 9, 1905—He primarily went by the name Henry, although in the first census report (1910 U.S. Census Report) he was enumerated showed his legal name as William Henry. Several documents discovered during my research showed he and my great-grandfather were referred to as Senior and Junior, affirming they had the same name and took the personal preference of dropping the William. Research of available records showed that he was not able to read and write. He married Ruth E. Spicer on April 3, 1926, and they had three children. When they separated, she remained in the house with her father-in-law and the kids. They never divorced. He later fathered a child, Emily Batts, with Essie Mae Batts. However, he and Essie Mae never married. He died of a sudden heart attack at the age of 45 on May 2, 1954, in New Bern, Craven County, North Carolina. He was living next door to his sister, my Aunt Bessie, at 608 Chapman Street in New Bern, North Carolina at the time of his death. He was buried in the Evergreen Cemetery in New Bern, North Carolina on May 9, 1954.

4th Bragg Generation Child No. 1, Parents: William Henry Jr. and Ruth: Fred Bragg, born February 1927.

4th Bragg Generation Child No. 2, Parents: William Henry Jr. and Ruth: James Ernest Bragg, born in 1928.

4th Bragg Generation Child No. 3, Parents: William Henry Jr. and Ruth: Edward Earl Bragg, my father, was born May 23, 1930, in North Carolina.

4th Bragg Generation Child No. 4, Parents: William Henry Jr. and Essie Mae Batts: Emily Batts, born December 27, 1933. She married Hosea Bradley, born May 1, 1922.

Fifth Bragg Generation - *Father Edward Earl Bragg*

Born in North Carolina, May 1930—Reflecting on this long line of blackberry seeds is moving, especially given the challenges facing African American men during the turn of the 19th and 20th centuries. Yet nothing stills my heart like the memory I have of that tall, dark, and handsome man coming down the street. The voice, the look, that special presence. Yep, that was my dad! This is a man who—despite his faults and failures—I am extremely proud to be deeply connected to his blackberry seed. Few days pass wherein I *don't* have a reflection on a probable conversation with my father. Absent of such critical discussions, I learned to endure many challenges based on having the next best thing—that he and I were both blessed to share the unadulterated love of my dear grandmother, Ruth. I have come to know great comfort in times of distress as a result of our relationship. One thing is for sure: love never fails; you can never go wrong following your heart. It never dawned on me to ask my parents what happened to their relationship—just as I never expect my children to inquire of me what happened between me and their mother. If you love your children, it's irrelevant. *I said love them.* That means they are still provided with everything they need to function in a healthy environment. For children of separated or divorced parents, it's important that communication is open, respectful, and honest. Children are never too young to talk to and be completely forthright with about what is happening. You just have to ***effectively*** communicate at their level.

I never knew my dad as an angry or violent man. I had only one minor encounter with him being upset. My daddy said to be quiet, and that was the end of the discussion. From this one occurrence, I gained a deep respect for his firm sense of discipline. It was effective and will forever reign in my mind. I knew he meant business, and I was not about to press my luck any further. I don't know if it was his particular and convincing command of the English language, his tone, deportment, or persuading voice. It is my most revered memory of a father's discipline imbued with the respect that accompanies the relationship. I see his unintentional likeness in my behaviors at times. I know that my children will wonder about these behaviors because they too are just like their Alphonso. Just ask their mothers; they will tell you it's the truth. They are too much like their daddy. It has been said a time or two that men seek out women who remind them of their mothers in some way. I somewhat agree. Like my father, I sought out these beautiful brazen gifts God had formed in his likeness. For the years I knew my father, he was separated from my mother. He and his companion Jackie lived on the South side of Wilmington on Orange Street. Grandma Ruth would take us to Wilmington to visit with him there, and I have fond memories of sitting on the front stoop enjoying a visit with my dad. He died on a Saturday morning, April 8, 1972, at New Hanover Memorial Hospital in Wilmington, North Carolina. The doctor said he had a stroke and did not get to the hospital in time. I recall the morning when the phone rang and we got the news he was in the emergency room waiting on someone to come over. That became the longest weekend of my life. He was buried in the Batts Cemetery near my sister and brother, and his brother Ernest.

5th Bragg Generation Child No. 1, Parents: Edward Earl and Idell: Anthony Lee Bragg, born June 11, 1951. He died from an electrocution accident on November 26, 1965. He was buried in the Browntown Community Cemetery.

5th Bragg Generation Child No. 2, Parents: Edward Earl and Idell: Earl Sherman Braggs, born December 4, 1952.

5th Bragg Generation Child No. 3, Parents: Edward Earl and Idell: Darita Annette Braggs, born November 19, 1953. She died of natural causes on December 3, 1953. She was buried in the Browntown Community Cemetery.

5th Bragg Generation Child No. 4, Parents: Edward Earl and Idell: Tyrone Romell Braggs, born February 28, 1955.

5th Bragg Generation Child No. 5, Parents: Edward Earl and Idell: Alphonso Braggs, born July 18, 1960.

5th Bragg Generation Child No. 6, Parents: Edward Earl and Idell: Alonzo Braggs, born July 18, 1960.

There are other children alleged to have been fathered by Edward Earl Bragg. **"Dad, why do they always believe we have other kids? I guess I understand. So, is it true?"** However, I was unable to ascertain sufficient legal evidence to document as fact.

"A Woman Named Ruth"

Although I heard disputes about her birth date, I understand Ruth Spicer was born in 1905 to Christopher and Martha Spicer. I still recall the stories she would tell of her childhood and the pride she instilled in us of our rich Native American (Cherokee) heritage. By the time I went to live with her, she was already a senior citizen who had raised two sons and was spending her golden years taking care of those two sons' families. I was too young to understand the circumstances. I just knew that her son, my daddy, had his kids living with her and her other son, Ernest, had his wife and kids also living with her also. It was a small place with a lot of people, but at that age none of that seemed to matter.

We all had different chores to perform based on our age and strength. The work was hard at times, but it was a part of living in the country. Grandma Ruth had a way of making everything work. During these early days I learned a lot about life. The most important lesson had to have been the golden rule for our home: *a loving family could face any situation and still come out victorious*. She taught us that our foundation and survivability was based on a bond of love that could not be broken. Moreover, it meant that we were never without because love has a way of filling empty voids like nothing else can do. When I was a kid, Grandma Ruth would tell me stories of our ancestors. I longed to meet them and was excited when I got to meet Aunt Bessie, Aunt Lula, and Uncle Miller. Of course, Cousin Joseph and Cousin Lucy were tremendously helpful in raising me. Likewise, I turned to Aunt Emily for a lot of support during those difficult teen years. I felt like Grandma Ruth was the perfect mom. There should be a book written on how to be a mother like Ruth Bragg. I know life must have been special growing up with her as a mom. It was certainly the case for me. I know that she gave my dad and uncle the same unconditional love we were given.

Trust me when I say that I really looked for women like Grandma Ruth to be the mother of my kids. As I have the opportunity to share with young couples and prospective husbands and fathers, I invoke the traits of Grandma Ruth as priceless inclusions for their successes. The core foundation of my mentoring is based on the life she lived. I would not have it any other way. I know she is proudly looking down from heaven smiling about how we are sharing her love to all mankind. Each day I ask myself, *"Dad, what more can I do to honor this virtuous woman?"* Listening to Grandma Ruth's stories and personally witnessing her strong faith and determination to live a righteous life and love humanity gave me the fortification I would later need to endure difficult times. I was barely old enough to walk and talk when I learned the story behind this wonderful woman named Ruth.

I remember Aunt Evalene, her sister, questioning her during one of her visits saying, "Ruth, how long they been calling you Grandma?" You see, we had been living with her since I was about six months old, and for a long time called her Mama. Only when we got older and learned differently did it change. Sadly, a few weeks before graduating from my U.S. Navy Yeoman "A" School, I got the news that she had passed on to glory. This was tremendously devastating to me. Ruth Bragg had raised me and taught me so much about life. No single individual has had so great an impact on my life or influenced my decision-making process. Many are familiar with the story of Boaz in the Old Testament of the Holy Bible, but I would contend that without his devoted helpmate Ruth, the world may never have known the greatness of David, the Wisdom of Solomon, or the other monumental blessings their offspring gave humankind. For me, I received a double blessing—the addition of a loving and devoted Grandma Ruth who epitomized the best representation of our family's legacy.

One of the primary reasons I aspired to succeed so early on in life was so that I could secure a permanent job and have a home where Grandma Ruth could spend the rest of her days. I could give back to her what she had given so graciously to me. I envisioned my kids coming home and running in the house to greet her and the fond memories they would have of her waving them off to school. My constant prayer was, *God, give me the ability to have a place to take care of Grandma Ruth.* I knew that having her near would give me another chance to learn more about being the best neighbor, father, husband, and family man. I would always be able to go to the source of the insurmountable and unconditional love and affection I came to find consolation in as a child. She had a unique and longstanding relationship with our family. Her influence expanded several generations and across family lines. She was selfless in so many ways except for her faith, which she shared regularly with any and all she encountered. Regardless of her changing situation, she made us her priority and ensured we were well taken care of. She was so beloved by neighbors, family, and friends. They simply saw a good woman doing her best to take care of those kids. At a time when most things in society were separated by race and economics, she became the classic exception. The movie *The Autobiography of Miss Jane Pittman* highlights the parallel between bigotry and respect. In the end, respect for the Godly woman Miss Pittman trumped the hatred shown. People put race aside and saw one of God's near-perfect creations simply trying to earn her Heavenly wings.

As a child I recall many occasions when she sacrificed for us. It was not uncommon for her to go without. In fact, many times she went without just to make sure that we had. Her faith devout and strong, and her daily petition to God for our well-being firm and constant. Her gentle voice and soothing comfort were a daily reassurance for anything I may have had to endure as a child. To this day, I rest in that comfort when I am confronted with great despair. Can I say that I have known so great a love as that shown by Grandma Ruth? Nay, I say! None! I really don't think that I could have made it this far without the great inspiration and strength I gained by reaching back on her wise counsel. She emphasized that it is important to know who we are and where we came from. This means fully understanding our human identity as well as the uniqueness of our African and Native American heritage. I am extremely proud of my upbringing and diverse heritage. I have been truly blessed to have the opportunity to sit in wise counsel with so many of my elders. As we would sit at her feet at the close of each day, she would read to us from the Holy Bible. She did more than just read. When she told those stories, it seemed like we were watching a major Hollywood production. She had infinite knowledge of the Holy Bible.

Yet, she never preached to us. She simply shared the stories and lived the principles the Holy Bible teaches. Somehow God and she had an arrangement that when it came time to share in the Holy Word, nothing from nature would disturb our precious learning time. I will always have fond memories of beautiful Saturday afternoons sitting in my neighbor's backyard learning about the word of God. Mrs. Naomi Moore, or Mama Naomi, as I called her, and her husband, Simon, were the first extended family members I came to know. It was the only place we were allowed to visit alone, and it was always a treat to go there. Usually in the summer we would go outside in the cool of the evening. Grandma Ruth would spread a cover down on the ground, and we would gather around. She pulled out the big family Bible, and we would be taught about the pictures and the stories. Then she would share about a particular scripture story, and we were forever captivated. We had no popcorn. We had no soda pop. Not even hot dogs or candy snacks. All we had was Grandma Ruth. We had a natural surround sound installed by God himself. Our temperature was regulated by the cool breezes sweeping through the trees and gently landing to comfort us without disturbing the pages of the Scriptures. Amazing how we got so filled on just her voice and presentation!

I feel sorry for the ones who did not regularly have this experience. The irony of being raised by Grandma Ruth is that I did not know that this activity was not normal. I had no clue that anything around us or about our situation was out of the ordinary. This is the difference a devout woman of God and a loving mother can make. She made our house a home—a real home where peace and love abound. In all my living days, I find it amazing that no matter how many people or situations I encounter, none make me see things differently. I attribute this resolve to the phenomenal power of peace she commanded for our home and surroundings. On top of all that love, she took the time to share with us golden treasures of our rich history. I gained a deeper appreciation of my ancestors' legacy through her moving stories of their lives. This made me very proud. It wasn't so much that they were great or popular. Instead, my pride came from being made to feel as though I knew them personally and felt connected. Through her stories, I was able to celebrate their successes and labor in their struggles. This bonding strengthened my vine. I got the sense that their lives had greater meaning and, therefore, I needed to ensure that my life also had a more profound meaning. I was able to understand my duty to enhance our legacy's value to mankind.

At appropriate times, we were blessed to hear from the other elders and members of the family. However, we also knew that just because there was a gathering, it was not an invitation for us kids to come running. To do so meant that you should expect an instant whipping, and it would surely be followed by a strong scolding and second whipping once company departed. Children knew their place, and we made sure we stayed there until we were summoned to appear before the wise and select, and to be blessed with their love, inspiration, and knowledge. Our days began and ended on our knees thanking God for what we had. Sometimes all we had was each other, but we still rejoiced. Funny how those times seemed to have been the best days of my life. Nothing else seemed to matter. How can this be? She would say, "We are safe in the hands of God!" I trusted her explicitly, and I knew she would never lie to us. Her untiring love and devout teaching of God's endless love proved itself over and over during those early years. Her profound words would be echoed and reinforced by the old country preacher when we would make our way to Browntown for Sunday services. Grandma Ruth showed us that even as a child you could handle the toughest crisis if you placed your faith in God. Whether she was dealing with the loss of her own children, my father and uncle, or struggling through severe illnesses, her faith never changed. The thing I remember most was the look in her eyes and her calming smile coupled with that reassuring soft voice. I was safe in her embrace, and the world from my perspective was okay.

I know that she was human because I saw her cry on several occasions. I don't mean to take anything away from Jesus when He cried out on the cross to His heavenly Father by comparing Him to Grandma Ruth. However, I relate how His commitment to His purpose and the pain He must have felt to that of the fervency and zeal that my Grandma Ruth had for loving and caring for her family and staying strong in her faith. Her greatest gift and lessons were her personal example of commitment to her grandchildren. At times I feel the only reason I live is to give back to society just a small portion of what she gave to us. I often tell people that no one loved me like Grandma Ruth. Likewise, no one would ever be able to shake the love she fostered in me for my father. Grandma Ruth taught me that no matter what, "Your father is still your father. Have a relationship with him." It is amazing how such a simple message can have such an enduring and empowering impact. I think it is primarily because I trusted unconditionally the words that she spoke. I had this unspeakable feeling that her words of counsel were directly from God and surely meant for me. Finally, I think it is because she was easy to believe and fate would prove her right time after time. Her message seemed to say his blood is my blood and he loves me. It is so important to tell your children you love them. What matters most is that they know and feel the love. However, you are still loved even if you don't hear the words spoken. Grandma Ruth made me understand that sometimes love exists even where it's not spoken. I believe her most important message was that children just want and need to be loved. I like the fact that she taught us it was okay to love those who are not perfect, and to not judge. It was because of God's grace and mercy that we were as good as we thought we were. This meant that we were no better than the common thief or any other criminal. She instilled an ethic that we could never go wrong by treating people right. I fondly recall when Grandma Ruth finally received her first social security check. I knew she was a senior citizen, but she never let her age stop her from whatever she had set her mind on to accomplish. Each month, Grandma Ruth would go to the post office and get her mail, and then she would take care of her bills. She had no bank account, so when the check came each month, she would dutifully cash it at the grocery store next door. The day after she cashed her check, we, along with her best friend, Naomi, got on the Trailways bus and headed to town. Grandma Ruth went shopping and purchased a new pink dress. She also bought a new pink dress for Mama Naomi. They wore them to church, and the folks had something to talk about. In all the years I lived with or knew my grandmother, this was the only time I had heard about anyone talking about her or gossiping. This taught me that we are all subject to human experiences.

When times were tough, Grandma would have these *whispered conversations* with the store manager and put stuff on credit at the store. She always took care of her bill when the check came. I now know as an adult looking back over the past what was meant for me to learn from *those* conversations. I would see the store owner ring up the few items of food and write my grandma's name on the back of the receipt. He would then place the receipt in his wallet. On the day when her social security check came in, he would pull out the receipts and give her the balance. Truly, these were trusting times, and nothing better personified the integrity and value of the saying, "A man's word is his bond." The interesting part is that Grandma Ruth never put special or big items on the bill. It was basic items like flour, sugar, salt, and a portion of meat for the Sunday meal. She was black, and the store owner was white, but her faith never wavered. She knew that God would have the store owner say yes, every time. Questions about the amount or a verification of the correct receipt never came up. It was just amazing. Grandma would take the time to share not only the stories of growing up and the cultural values she experienced but also the tremendous joy that comes from passing on this rich cultural heritage. She often emphasized that it is ***not the famous but the familiar*** who will carry forth this great legacy.

"A Foundation of Faith and Fortitude"

There is not a day that passes that I do not draw on the strengths of my religious upbringing. From my early childhood, the church has played a key role in my life. I have many instances where I came to that "fork" in the road while traveling down this "highway of life." I was able to get back on the right path only because of the wonderful preachers, teachers, and caring Christians in my life. It was during gravely troubling times that I came to appreciate the wisdom and guidance of fervent church leaders. We were always a family centered on faith. Looking at our family, I see so many examples of hardship and trauma. I know the only thing that got us through these times was our faith in God. I am so glad that Grandma Ruth gave us a foundation based on a strong belief in God. When my oldest brother, Anthony Lee, died, it really hurt Grandma Ruth. I felt like I lost my best friend. He was the perfect person in my eyes, and I knew no kinder person other than Grandma Ruth. Then we lost Uncle Ernest. She was devastated. Somehow, she managed to still put others first and celebrate a true and living God. These are just two examples of loss and troubling times.

I am here today to enjoy my children and grandchildren because of the love I received from those in the church. I was born in Wilmington, North Carolina, and our family lived in Jervay projects. However, shortly thereafter we moved, and I was raised on a small plot of land in Hampstead, Pender County, North Carolina. Times were tough, but we were loved, healthy, and devout. We never let the day begin without thanking God for all His wonderful blessings. Likewise, we would not end our day without taking the time to say thanks to God for bringing us through another day. Our religious development wasn't limited to learning just at our house. Good upbringing came from the whole neighborhood and even school leaders. There were two churches to attend in

Browntown. One was Christian Chapel, where my mother's side of the family held membership, and the other was St John, where my daddy's side of the family held their membership. Although the families were from different church denominations, they got along well and held their services on different Sundays in the month. The preachers were called circuit preachers because they held services on fixed Sundays over a large area covering churches. Most Sundays, members attended each other's church programs. Grandma Ruth was a member of St John's Disciples of Christ Church in Browntown, Pender County, North Carolina. Browntown was a little community just up the road from Hampstead. All the people I came to know as members of my family were church folks. Going to church was like having a Sunday family reunion. I learned that so many of my elders were staunch Bible believers, and their practices helped me to build a strong religious foundation.

While I was living with Grandma Ruth, we witnessed numerous incidents that tested her faith. We also witnessed her deal with multiple health challenges. Still, God brought us through. Nothing seemed to shake her faith or that of our family. My children were raised with the same faithful trust. They have been taught that there may be times when they feel like all they have is God. They, like their father, have encountered situations that forced them to get down on bended knees and cry out for relief and comfort. In the tradition of our elders, we will keep the faith and resolve that this is our fate. We will be grateful that God has chosen our family to prove His promise to the faithful. We moved to Grandma Ruth's house with the help of our Cousin Ruth (Grandma Ruth's Sister Evalene daughter and namesake). According to my Brother Earl, she packed the kids in her 1957 station wagon and took us to the country. He went on to share that to help with the twin babies, the two oldest brothers (Anthony Lee and Earl) were each responsible for a twin. I was assigned to Earl. I am so glad that no one saw my reaction when I came into this knowledge. I was completely overwhelmed. I have always admired Earl from afar and privately aspired to achieve as he has done. I guess now I know why.

My brothers did their best to see that we had a good life while growing up in Hampstead, North Carolina. I remember one year they got a basketball. They took a bicycle rim and nailed it to the side of the house. That was the first time I recall my big brothers trying to teach their little brothers how to play sports. Many years later, I recall Earl picking up where he left off and inviting us to come down to the basketball court in the Jervay projects where we lived. The Wills family owned the house we lived in with Grandma Ruth. As a child, I recall my grandmother tending to the elder Mrs. Wills. Living with Grandma out in the country gave me all the freedom to run and roam. I saw wild animals and enjoyed living off the land. Next to Hampstead was Browntown and it was named after our maternal side of the family. Whenever one family had a situation, the entire community had a situation. The two things that kept us deeply connected were church and school. Our elders believed too much had been sacrificed for us to pass up getting an education. So, we did not take going to school and getting good grades for granted. What we learned in school was reinforced at home and church. All of our teachers were believers, and we had prayer and got whippings as needed. Between prayer and the paddle, we got the lessons learned and the grades were okay to take home. You see, those devout teachers who worshiped with us on Sunday morning did not hesitate to invoke the power of God or the persuasion of the paddle during the week.

I went to a segregated school for the first three grades at Annandale Elementary School in Topsail, North Carolina. Until we integrated, this was the only school the Black kids attended. It had eight classrooms separated by a folding partition. When we needed to hold an assembly, we would all gather in Mr. Wilson's and Mr. McGee's combined class space. It was not uncommon to run into one of the teachers at a family gathering or at church. Students had to be careful not to get into trouble, or they would be swiftly dealt with. Annandale was desegregated by the time I attended the fourth grade. I didn't really notice racial tensions in school until I attended the fifth grade at Topsail Middle and High School in Hampstead. My maternal great-grandmother, Hattie Brown Nixon, belonged to Christian Chapel. She lived next door to our church, St John. So anytime we went to church, we always would stop by to see Mama Hattie (that's what all the grands and great-grands called her). She was one of the oldest living persons in our family. A road lay between Mama Hattie's house and St John's church. It was the entryway into a near-perfect square field. Along the field borders were houses, occupied by our family. Right behind Mama Hattie's house lived her daughter, my aunt, Mildred Hansley. We called her Aunt Sissy. She mostly resembled Mama Hattie in stature and behavior.

Mama Hattie's brother, my uncle, Mr. Jessie Brown, lived at the back of the field. He lived to be 102 years old. In the summer, the community would have lots of games, fish frys, and family reunions. It is interesting to recall the small stretch of road that Mama Hattie lived on. The road ran parallel to the main interstate, Highway 17. The original name for that stretch of road in Browntown was Newbern Road. The land that the family houses sit on was originally purchased by my Great-Great-Grandmother Caroline Powell Brown (Mama Hattie's mom). The land was purchased from the Singleton family in Hampstead, North Carolina. While researching records to write this book, I was amazed at the value of homes in Browntown that were owned by my family during the early 20th century. The reported value of Great-Great-Grandma Caroline's home was $1,000, whereas Mama Hattie's home was valued at $250. "Mamie," as she was called, was a midwife and married my Great-Great-Grandfather Ephraim Brown when she was 13. He was born in Harrison Creek, North Carolina and was much older than she. The land she purchased was divided so that each of their children had a plot.

Between the front road and the highway was a railroad track. On this road lived (at least in my opinion) a group of elder women who were the perfect example of holy and devout living. Church mothers like Aunt Laura Brown, Rosa Sidberry, Georgina Brinson, and Hattie Nixon are hard to find. The houses from Aunt Laura Brown to Mama Hattie were built by the Brown men under the leadership of Uncle Ephraim Brown. We grew up revering these ladies, and we entered into their presence with a Godly fear and reverential awe. Mrs. Georgina's son-in-law, Willie McGee, and his wife, Evangelist McGee, were teachers. Mr. McGee taught at the Annandale School and drove the school bus for the students who lived on our side of the county. No one walked down that stretch of road without giving due regard to those old sisters. By that I mean that your walk had to properly represent your family and Christian upbringing. You also paid particular attention to your manners. These ladies would sit on their front porch, and as you passed you made sure you paid proper respect. God knows you had better not get a bad report card sent home or have one of them to call you out for something. These ladies had the same standards for each of us, regardless of our age. I recall visiting with Mrs. Sidberry in the summer of 2004. At 106, she remembered who I was from way back when. One day when I stopped by, she abruptly summoned me to her side. She sternly took my hand and, after smacking it a few times, stated that it had been too long since I stopped by to see her, and to not let it happen again.

Reflecting on that precious moment of love exchanged, I can barely contain myself, because few will ever experience this rare discipline or comprehend its tremendous cultural and moral value. That day I made sure to video our visit. We sat and talked for over an hour. Sadly, she passed a few months later. She was the last of these Browntown Church mothers who lived on that front road. Grandma Ruth made sure we knew these women. I can honestly say that my life was richly blessed because of their personal examples and spiritual influences. On the other side of St John Church lived Cousin Arnold Brown and his wife Beatrice. He was my Uncle Jesse's son. Their granddaughter, Michelle, and I were in the same grade. We were taught by another family member in the third grade, Cousin Rosetta Brown, my fourth cousin. Cousin Rosetta's grandfather, Ephraim, is Mama Hattie's brother. She was the sweetest teacher that I had my entire time going to school. On the other side of Cousin Arnold's house is a plot of land that the elders said was donated to the family for a cemetery.

The first family member to be buried there was Uncle Dave Batts. Thus, the name of the cemetery is Batts Cemetery. He married into the family. His wife Mary Batts and my Great-Great-Grandmother Caroline Brown were sisters. It is the final resting place for my mother's father. It was Uncle Needham Brown who filed the paperwork with the coroner upon the death of my Grandfather Porter Nixon. He was the oldest of Mama Hattie's children, and my mother was her first of 53 grandchildren. Mama Hattie's Brother Needham was married to Aunt Laura. My grandfather died at the age of 21 when my mother was only a few years old. All of the men in the family gravitated to my mom and assisted in her rearing and support for life. In retrospect, one can draw a parallel between my mother and I internalizing our emotions on dealing with the early and traumatic loss of our fathers. A deeper look into the parallel corridors and one can see how we have been closely drawn and taken care of by our father's side of the family. A special deference was given to each of us. I had not taken the time to consider this fact until I began to research this book.

My mother was the catalyst who kept the family fighting to survive. Over the years my mother has had to endure the loss of a newborn daughter, a teenage son, and an adult son who went missing back in the mid-1980s—all of this as well as health issues, socioeconomic challenges, loss of loved ones, and the burdens of trying to keep a dysfunctional family functional. Despite all these challenges, she never gave up hope that things would be better and different for her kids. She undoubtedly was a survivor. Even in her golden years when she was not able to move as quickly or attend activities as she would have liked, she still commanded a powerful sting in her "whip." Likewise, her mind was as sharp as an eagle's talon. It is easy to see why she—bold, brazen, and seasonally beautiful—was chosen to bear these blackberry seeds. I came from a large family, both immediate and extended, with lots and lots of aunts, uncles, and cousins. Like most families, we experienced personal tragedies. Grandma Ruth told us stories of how my mother lost her dad when she was a baby. Somehow these tragedies drew us closer to God. When I was young, around the age of five, I lost my oldest brother, Anthony Lee. He was accidentally electrocuted during a fishing trip with my Uncle Ernest.

I can never forget that morning. I was outside alone playing in the road when I saw him approaching from afar. I vividly recall the clarity of the sun piercing through the country trees as the morning began to unfold. I recall seeing Uncle Ernest hurrying to the house and asking for Grandma. I sensed he had something important on his mind, but I felt ignored because he did not answer me. I kept asking, "Where is Nantny?" As a child, I could not pronounce his whole name, so I called him Nantny. This was one of the longest days for our family and the community. People began to gather at the house well into the night, patiently waiting to hear how the beloved young boy had fared. Sadly, the news came that he did not make it through the day. His body could not endure the trauma. I recall the elders saying the live wire fried him and his skin looked like a baked potato. I was devastated. What was I to do? He was my favorite. **"Dad, how did his loss make you feel."** I was not that old. However, I was old enough to understand **"permanent"** loss and feel the absence of a brother I loved dearly. He was so much like my dad, and he helped my grandma around the house and with raising us boys. This was a sobering time for our family. I felt Anthony was the best person in the world, and everyone loved him. A few years later, I also lost my daddy's only living brother, Uncle Ernest.

When my Uncle Ernest died, I recall the day of the funeral. My twin brother and I were dropped off at Mama Hattie's house while the rest of the family went to town for the funeral. The day was special for a number of reasons: one, we got to spend quality time with Mama Hattie; and two, she took care of us in a special way and allowed us to attend the service. Mama Hattie found some of our older cousins' clothes, dressed us up, and walked us down to the Batts cemetery where the burial took place. Grandma Ruth was surprised to see us all dressed up in our cousins' clothes, but happy that we were able to attend. Losing family members like my brother and uncle without losing faith are perfect examples of how Grandma Ruth taught us to handle life's most challenging times. In each instance of death, sickness, or trauma, she pressed on, never forgetting, or losing her strong faith in God or her commitment to developing our spiritual being. She taught us that if we keep the faith, things will get better. She never complained and encouraged us to remain optimistic. She reminded us that we would see our brother again if we lived correctly. I now understand why. Grandma Ruth felt that God's Word was very important and held frequent bible studies with us. I also remember the extended family bible studies she would have at our house. It seemed like we would have family members and friends travel from miles and miles to attend. The house would be full. I was too young to really understand the importance of bible study then, but the development of good study practices would remain with me for life.

Grandma Ruth's sister, Aunt Martha, lived in Onslow County. She would bring other family members and church members down on Saturdays for a day-long visit and bible study. They would bring food and caravan in several cars. When I was about ten years old, we moved back to Wilmington, North Carolina to live with my mother. Wilmington was my birth town and was located in the next county, New Hanover. There I would complete my young adult religious development and endure even more painful tragedies. When I arrived in Wilmington, it was a while before I got back into church, and it took a long time to get used to the change in living arrangements. City life was totally different from the freedom of the country. People were not as friendly, and I was uncomfortable with making friends. This was a new experience and way of living. One of the great joys of moving to the city, though, was finally meeting my maternal grandmother, Rosabell Nixon Hansley. As I did with my paternal grandmother, I became close to Grandma Rosabell and treasured each moment we spent together. She loved her twins. She would call us and say, "Twin, Grandma made some tea if you want some" or "Grandma made a cake."

Grandmothers, for me, have always been a great place of comfort. They just seem to know what to say to make everything okay. Grandma Rosabell also introduced me to a lot of other relatives I had not yet met. I knew well Grandma Rosabell's brothers who lived in Hampstead and Scotts

Hill. We would run into them at church or when the family came together on various occasions. Grandma Ruth had told us stories about the many yet-to-meet uncles, aunts, and cousins. The dots were beginning to connect, and I was excited. As the family tree began to blossom, one of them, Margaret Simmons, would become a lifelong anchor. I had not met Cousin Margaret before moving to Wilmington. However, her sister Lillian and her husband Eugene were remarkably close to my Grandma Ruth. We worked on their tobacco farm. Grandma Ruth would tell me that we were related on my mother's side. Grandma Rosabell's father and Cousin Margaret's father were brothers. Cousin Margaret's mom lived to see 100 years. All attribute the family's longevity to good genes and faithful living. Next to Grandma Ruth, no other woman in my opinion walked so close to God. She was a member of St Andrew African Methodist Episcopal Zion Church, and we soon began attending church with her. It did not take long for us to become hooked on "Zion." When I visited her in the early summer of 2004, she sang her testimony song and allowed me to video the performance.

Her voice was still very strong at the ripe age of 84. She knew the words and showed great comfort singing them. We visited many times over the years, and she shared stories of our family. She was one of the few who helped me better understand my father and the ***unique*** encounters of his life. ***"Dad, she had the firsthand goods on you."*** When I moved to Wilmington, I missed my Grandma Ruth a lot, and within a year, my father passed. These events and various problems with adjusting to a new environment made me a troubled youth. Now I know that even at that young age, my religious foundation was being tested; while I was beginning to explore the various "highways of life," I would never recover from the loss of my father. To this day, I don't think I ever grieved the way I needed to. For some reason during that period of my life, I was unable to show much emotion about a lot of things. Somehow, I just didn't feel free to share. I also felt as though no one would understand these things the way Grandma Ruth would, so I kept them to myself. My outlets were school, where I was often disruptive, and church. It seems I was happiest at church. I tried to make it my business to be there anytime the church doors were open. I found out that I loved the business of church as well as the spiritual uplifting that the worship experience provided. We sang, ushered, participated in numerous programs, and eventually held offices. I really enjoyed the youth programs, singing, and community service activities.

I gained my greatest self-esteem from Grandma Ruth and the time I spent in the church. I clung to those who embodied the same qualities as Grandma Ruth. I sought their sage wisdom and yielded to their firm counsel. I was inspired by those with character traits like Mama Hattie and the others elders from Browntown and Scotts Hill. Anytime I could gain a little of what I had lost by moving to Wilmington, I would take hold of it and latch on to it for dear life. The church became an excellent place for learning and gaining pride in my rich African American and Native American heritages. There were great men of the AME Zion Church like Bishop Herbert Bell Shaw Sr., Presiding Elder E. S. Hassell, and Rev. Robert W. Johnson who saw to it that I was deeply rooted in the Gospel and properly trained in Methodism. I had great admiration for the kindred spirit that existed among the leaders. I saw it often when I attended Sunday evening fellowships with various church denominations or when we had AME Zion workshops and meetings. I didn't know exactly what it was, but I knew a deep bond and respect for each other existed; it kept me wanting to learn more and become more involved.

I found great joy being trained in religious and civic leadership and development by Posey Johnson, Margaret Simmons, and Katie Goode. There was nothing that they could ask of me that I would not eagerly do. I took advantage of every leadership conference, seminar, and workshop to learn how to lead, teach, organize, and direct church business and people. Some of these ladies and gentlemen had that special gift to teach and make you want to learn. It was just a special treat for me to be in their company, and the added value was that I could learn from them. Looking back, I am sure they were simply fulfilling the tenants of the old gospel song entitled, "Use Me Lord, In Thy Service." Under their astute instruction, I learned church organization, doctrine, and finance. They also taught me the great value of caring for people. Moreover, I learned that during uncertain times, this was one of the institutions that held strong.

I wonder if Rev. Johnson knew when he appointed me a junior trustee that some two decades later, I would serve as a full trustee at the historic First AME Zion Church in San Francisco, California. The loving support and inspiration of Mrs. Johnson and Mrs. Goode to organize the local and District Youth Council and serve as its president launched my career in public service and affirmed my passionate desire to help improve humanity. I wonder if they knew that their mentoring would make such a huge difference in the life of this troubled young man! How I wish they could peek in on me now and know just how grateful I am for their investment in my life and well-being. Their influences and teachings made it far beyond this pupil. Yes, on this road of life, it has been my great honor to pass on some of their fine instructions. My daily prayer was for God to richly bless each of them for being an instrument of His use. Devout women such as Mrs. Simmons (my church class leader) and Mrs. Johnson (my Sunday School Teacher) instilled in me a great love for Zion, its future, and most importantly, how to love its people. They showed me how to have selfless love in serving God and others. Their pride in religious stewardship is now my pride. Their example is now my example of servant leadership. I embody their teachings and love. It is going to be exceedingly difficult for anyone to diminish the hold they have on my commitment. I do not think that Bertha Todd, Margaret Williams, Margaret Baham, or Connie B. O'Dell (high school mentors and counselors) realized that engaging me outside of the schoolhouse would have such a profound impact. They invited me to share in their civic and religious activities around the city.

Even after high school, I was invited back to their homes and made to feel a special part of their lives. I fondly reflect on them and hold dear those precious memories. Other strong men and women of faith at each of my schools helped me navigate this course of life. I am grateful to those who took the extra time to show me a better way of life and, most importantly, helped me to discover my purpose. I cannot conclude this section without reflecting on the unnamed ancestors and the amazing struggle I now understand they endured—their journey from Africa, their ill treatments in this new land, and the difficult challenges they faced trying to make a better place for future generations. I am reminded of that old prayer that speaks of their abiding faith and devout commitment to my future success. The truth is that we have been resting in the hands of God for longer than we have existed.

"Sustained by Grace"

I loved my time at St. Andrew AME Zion Church and felt that it gave me the proper training and preparation for my adult Christian life. After graduating from high school, I joined the U.S. Navy at the age of seventeen and left Wilmington. Following basic training in Orlando, Florida, and advanced in-rate training in Meridian, Mississippi, I finally settled down in Washington, DC. I lived in the military barracks located on the historic Fort Myer Army Base. I enjoyed being stationed at our nation's capital, but something was missing. After a few years at Fort Myer, several young Christian military members got together and organized the Fort Myer Gospel Service. Rev. Gene Walton served as our first lay leader. Rev. Walton was in the Army and worked with the Chaplains at Fort Myer. Most of us did not have cars, so we ended up staying on post. Having a church that we were culturally and spiritually familiar with made a substantial difference and provided a permanent spiritual anchor in our young lives.

This was the best thing and the closest I got to real home church. We were all young service members and young in the Lord. It was a great time for us all, and we could relate to the challenges of being young, black, and saved. Rev. Walton had that down-home style that I was used to, and I was not homesick anymore for friends, family, or, most importantly, God's Word. We held our weekly services in the historic Fort Myer Chapel. During the week we went to bible study at the main chapel. We were a strong support group for each other. It is amazing to look back and see how far we have come. Many in our group have gone on to establish their own churches or hold prestigious positions in places of worship across the country. The main message that Rev. Walton preached was that the lessons we were learning were not for the present. Rather, we were being groomed for the future. He would often remind us not to get too comfortable with our little Fort Myer social setting. We all started out as a bunch of singles from different branches of service, dependents, and civil service. We formed into a truly devout fundamental religious family. We had a powerful choir, usher board, prayer warriors, and team of ministers. Pretty soon we were known around town and began fellowshipping with local churches and appearing on their Sunday programs. It was great to witness people enjoying themselves in the service of the Lord no matter what their rank or position in life. This was a humbling and developing time for us all. I'm reminded of the gospel song entitled, "I'm A Soldier in the Army of the Lord." We were all soldiers in the military from different branches. I fondly remember wonderful fellowships with James Wiggins, Army; Ann Miller, Navy; Darnel Strick, Army; and Fred Clarke, Army; along with Karla from the Air Force. Likewise, we will never forget Carlton's dynamic voice. He was Army affiliated. The list of people I could name just goes on. The wonderful memories shared with so many people—so many faces, and many of their names escape me now—will never be forgotten. We had so many great times at church, home, and around town.

We began to band together into small little families within the church. Bruce James, his wife Vera, Darnel Strick, and I became particularly good friends. I soon met Fred Clark, Sammy James, and his wife Tracy. I cannot forget about Sgt Thomas and his wife Brenda or Mac Graham and his wife Shirley with her sister Eva Jo. These were my "Old Guard" buddies. Bruce was in my wedding and is a lifetime friend. Of course, we had two Fred Clarks representing the Army. One was in the Old Guard and the other one worked in the Army personnel office on base. One of my most coveted pleasures was ushering on Sundays with the two Freds. Not to be outdone, the Air Force equally contributed to our core group with Faye, Barbara, Sandy, Trudy, Cathy, Viola, Lil' Mike, Dewayne, and his wife, and so many others. We were mindful of our military status and kept our work relations professional. However, we were realistic, and as a church family we did things together. Most would agree Ann Miller was the head of the Navy team when she became part of our inseparable group. We had Robert, Bobby, Iris, Marsha, Ken, and Mike. There were countless others. Ann's roommate Jackie was our second in command. It was our belief that even though we were Christians, we could still have fun.

The great Hollywood scriptwriters could not come up with a story as great as our Sunday afternoon church events. We were spread out all over the capital region. Most of us worked at the Pentagon, so we also got to see each other during the workday. We always managed to find each other at the end of the workday and more than likely had something planned to keep us going on the weekends.

One of the many fun things we did was planning outings at different locations along the East Coast. From time to time we would have small fellowships and bible studies in the barracks. The interesting point here is that we were all in the prime of our young adult life. We were dealing with religious convictions and peer pressure to do things contrary to our religious teachings. Life was so much easier because of the strength and support from our core group. On payday weekends we would dress up and have dinner at some of the nice restaurants around the nation's capital. A large group of us would even go to the nearby amusement parks. After some of the group began to marry off and get their own houses, we began to enjoy home-cooked meals. It wasn't long before we were all godparents as the church and its families began to grow both in numbers and also in the Gospel. However, when we got back to our barracks with all the regular guys, temptation would bring on its full challenges. It was good that we had several members living in our barracks who we could go to and discuss what was going on with each of us during this period of our lives.

It was also helpful to work near each other during the week so that we could gain that emotional support during the week. Each week, we added new members to the fold. Most of us were inviting friends from the barracks to join us in the service. We also got a lot of the newly reporting service members. As our church grew, so did our programs. We expanded our service to include youth church, men's fellowship, women's fellowships, and overnight pray-ins. Our small ministry team grew to several members, and so did our music ministry. We had a large portion of the congregation enroll and graduate in a theology class taught at the chapel. The church was well on its way. It was soon pointed out to us that we were the second largest congregation on post and second also in offerings. While we could not function totally as a civilian church, we were given a lot of flexibility to conduct our Gospel Service in the tradition of the African American church. The feedback across the post validated the effectiveness our service was having on its congregation. God's purpose for our young group was being fulfilled. We were formally organized into a parish structure, and officers were elected. I served as Vice President of the Church Board.

I was passing through the barracks one day and ran into a Solder by the name of Rev. John Williams. It turns out his church was having a revival that coming Friday, and he invited me.

This encounter began my affiliation with Rev. Barbara Vaughn and the host of wonderful folks at Holy Light United Baptist Church. Rev. Williams lived in my barracks and worked at the Army Personnel Office as a supervisor issuing identification cards. He was from South Carolina and, in my humble opinion, played the piano like no other I had encountered. He was also a gifted singer and great preacher. I soon made the transition from the Fort Myer Gospel Service to Holy Light church, located in Merrifield, Virginia. Because I required transportation to attend services, Rev. Williams would often give me a ride to and from church. He introduced me to a lovely young sister in the Army medical field named Celeste Samuels. She instantly became my church sister.

Nothing compared to the down-home services we had at Holy Light. It was so much like being home. Everyone was so inviting, and spirit filled. No foolishness there! I became very close to our Pastor, Rev. Vaughn, and had the utmost respect and admiration for her husband, Trustee George Vaughn. He became my church father. We had an incredibly special mother in the church by the name of Mother Clifton. She was such a lady of class! Everything, including her devout faith, reflected a state of royalty and elegance. She was a fine example of a lady for the young ladies and kept the young men on their toes when it came to how a gentleman should treat a lady. When Mother Clifton spoke, we all listened and obeyed. When I came to the church it was relatively new, and she was one of the original members of the church. Rev. Williams inspired me to join the male chorus, and he was our accompanist. I enjoyed singing with the male chorus at Holy Light and even got to lead a few songs. Pastor Vaughn's daughter was also a minister and served as the church organist. She could set the church on fire with her mastery of the keyboard and vocal praises. We had a host of great singers including Larry, Cathy, and Celeste.

Within a year, I would transfer from the Military District Washington to Groton, Connecticut. I spent the rest of my time between Holy Light and Fort Myer Gospel Service. The spiritual foundation I got there as an adult has sustained me to this day. For the next twenty years I served almost exclusively on sea duty and didn't attend as regularly as I would have liked or needed. However, I was blessed to find a church home at each duty station and did manage to anchor down with the congregation. I arrived in Groton, Connecticut new to the North and the culture. The greatest comfort came in having my new wife there and finding an African Methodist Episcopal Zion church to attend. We started attending Walls Temple African Methodist Episcopal Zion

Church under the leadership of Rev. Donald W.H.E. Ruffin. Again, the Savior was listening to the elders' fervent prayers and connected me to a church with a familiar form of worship. Even more important, He placed me in a congregation led by a pastor who left no doubt about his spiritual ability. I spent a little more than five years at the base. The first three years, I was constantly at sea. Unlike Fort Myer, the congregation gave me everything that I had back at home growing up. Fort Myer was great; however, it was mostly just young adults. At Walls Temple we had elders, children, neighborhoods—everything just like home. Of course, I found another church mom, Connie Chapman. She took care of my family and me the whole time we were there and became great friends with our families down South. I also met my future sister-in-law, Laurice. She would become my dear friend and trusted confidant. We were family long before she met and married my twin brother. My wife, Cathy, was responsible for connecting the two of them. Whenever there was a chance to fellowship, I was at her home. I always had a home for the holidays and a prayer partner, should I needed to talk or pray. It was also at Walls Temple that I met Rev. Florence Clark and her husband George, a fellow submariner.

Rev. Clark and Rev. Barbara Harris were great mentors for both Cathy and me. Rev. Clark and Rev. Harris were our other church leaders at Walls Temple. They worked together to keep us on the straight and narrow and always saw to our spiritual and emotional needs. I sang in the male chorus at Walls Temple, and one of my most memorable moments was meeting Bro. George Clark. I showed up for rehearsal one Saturday morning and humbly introduced myself to Bro. Clark for the first time. Quite an imposing but kind gentleman, he inquired about my career. When I responded that I was just arriving to the submarine service, he quickly replied, "non-qual, huh." I will never forget that "inside" meaning as he was reminding me about the respect and deference that existed between a "qualified" and a "nonqualified" submariner. I still laugh about that greeting to this day.

We had other Submarine brothers in the choir, Charlie Matchen and Loston Powell. Bro. Matchen was a retired Submarine Yeoman. I loved working with the church leadership at Walls Temple. I was given the honor of being the guest speaker for one of Rev. Clark's Sunday afternoon programs. This was another affirmation that no matter where we go in life, opportunities exist; for me, most have come from the church. The journey of special people placed in our paths continued when we left Groton, Connecticut and moved to Alameda, California. In the Bay area, I joined First African Methodist Episcopal Zion Church under the leadership of Rev. John E. Watts and his lovely wife Geneva Watts. They immediately took us under their wings and helped us become the young man and woman of Christ we were destined to become. Rev. Watts was instrumental in officiating Cathy's transition into the ministry and mentored us both in Christian discipleship. Just as I experienced tremendous love and nourishment on the East Coast, I felt the same on the West Coast. I saw my grandma and other family members in the faces and spirits of the beautiful saints at First Church. Cathy and I were so happy to have Rev. and Mrs. Watts as our spiritual anchors. I was blessed to serve in several capacities at First Church including the Board of Trustees, Usher Board, Choir, Lay Council, and Men's Christian Fellowship. Not many folks know that my favorite place to serve in the church is the usher's board. I feel a special honor being able to welcome the saints to the house of worship. The way First Church was designed added to the special feeling that one experienced—walking in off the street and having to look up high and ascend the steps to get into the main sanctuary.

The military took me from San Francisco, California to Honolulu, Hawaii. God had a plan to bring me back a few years later, and I was blessed to spend more time with my church family. I did not have transportation, so Rev. and Mrs. Watts saw to it that I did not miss a meeting or a worship service. I worked on Mare Island Naval Shipyard in Vallejo, California. Mrs. Watts was the elementary school principal at Mare Island Naval Shipyard. It was great to stop by from time to time to see my mentor at work. They would come on base and pick me up, and we would make the journey to the city. Something as simple as a car ride afforded us the best opportunities to build relationships and enrich our spiritual bond. I can't recall a trip where they did not share in helping to build on my spiritual and intellectual foundation. I always grew as a man and person of faith from our Sunday rides. Sometimes they would play the good cop/bad cop treatment with me while teaching me life lessons. Usually, it was Mrs. Watts who would come to my rescue. One Sunday morning Rev. Watts made a comment about my Grandma Ruth. It struck a nerve with me, and I became emotional. He didn't see my reaction. She said, "John, I think you hurt Alphonso's feelings." With the loving and compassionate wisdom of a mother, Mrs. Watts gently and promptly redirected the discussion and restated how the discussion should have gone. I am forever in her debt. Special times at First Church also included the quarterly and annual conferences. We seemed to host our fair share of special events. We had a few Zion churches in the area. We were the only one in San Francisco, and there were two in Oakland and one located in Vallejo. Likewise, I enjoyed making the journey down to San Jose and Pala Alto for services or attending Lay Council sessions in Oakland with Rev. Keith Harris and his congregation. Cathy and I initially attended churches on the Oakland side but eventually settled on becoming a member at First Church.

While I was at First Church, I had a secret prayer partner on the Usher Board. She seemed to know when things were not going well and in her motherly way she would gently approach and give me that affirmation that all was in God's hand. Much like my grandma, I knew no matter what she was calling my name when she went down on bended knees at the close of day. I gained so much respect and admiration for many of the members and felt a special bond with families like the Rochons, who took me in as their own. My dear friend Joyce Shepherd and her family were a constant source of comfort and inspiration. Over the years I watched the kids from the church grow to become young men and women of success with families of their own. The friendships continued to grow. Most of all, the memories never faded.

When I moved to Honolulu, Hawaii, I was very sad to learn that we did not have an African Methodist Episcopal Zion church in the state. I began to worship at Trinity Missionary Baptist Church in Honolulu, Hawaii during periods I wasn't deployed. As was the case with my other seaports, it was a great comfort to have the church here and know that my family had trusted friends and people to call on in time of crisis. Living in paradise is wonderful. Folks had church outside on the beach or anywhere outdoors on a regular basis. Until I retired, I did not attend church as much. There were attempts in years past and most recently an endeavor to establish an AME Zion presence in the islands. Although I never officially joined the church, I have affectionately considered Trinity Missionary Baptist Church my church home in Hawaii, and I love the church family. Most of the members and I are friends and see each other regularly. As much as possible, I attend their special programs and activities sponsored by my civic and fraternal organizations. Yes, God has been good to me and my family. His abiding grace and mercy have kept us from all hurt, harm, or danger. As I anchor into the fall season of life, I'm blessed to be black, saved, just a bit older, and still working for the government!

"An Island and a Man"

No man is an island! Should life on an island cease to exist and is washed away with the sands of time, history will still record the fact that "this is an island." However, on the other hand, a man is a fool if he thinks he can continue to survive without recognizing the very existence of those responsible for his present place in history. Man continues to exist because he recognizes that somewhere somehow someone needs or wants some application or extraction, he is able to provide. The laws of supply and demand are simple to understand. Discourage the need or want for your existence and you will die! No man is an island!

Alphonso Braggs

"Singing Zion's Song"

It's a typical Sunday morning at Walls Temple African Methodist Episcopal Zion Church located in New London, Connecticut. The Zion Ensemble is marching down the aisle singing one of the great processional hymns of the African American church. I am sure that we were not the only church starting our service to the tune of "Marching to Zion." With Sister Evelyn Ruffin on the piano and Brother Charlie Matchen taking the lead, the tone was set for what is traditionally called in the African American church, a "high time in the Lord."

We're marching, marching up to Zion; that beautiful city of God.
We're marching, marching up to Zion; that beautiful city of God.

This song had a way of lifting your heart and soul to a higher place where you are traveling on to Glory. Walls Temple, like most churches, gave soul-stirring performances much like the powerful Ruth Davis and the Famous Davis Sisters of Philadelphia, Pennsylvania who were known for electrifying their audiences. I am totally taken by their version of this beloved song with Sis. Imogene Green on the lead. That was until I ran across a spirited rendition with Bro. Eugene Smith leading the Famous Roberta Martin Singers of Chicago, Illinois, and I have yet to determine which I consider the best. *"Sing Choir!"* you could hear an old sister shout as the choir processed her way. *"March on children,"* an elder may utter as they swayed and moved down the aisle.

Just the thought of such a song and the memory of being there can ease a heavy heart. This great processional depicts the Christian's journey from earth to glory. Along the way Christians have encountered many struggles and heavy burdens. Nevertheless, they are encouraged along the way. This philosophy has always been evident in the prolific manner African Americans have sung the great gospel songs. Although Sister Ruffin was a fine pianist, she was no match for Sister Coleen Lee, the pianist for the male chorus at Walls Temple. She made a piano do things only a few would attempt. These songs sung in the African American church were delivered with such fervor and power; they could have easily incited a riot. At least, that's one man's opinion of the "power" both the song and the singer could generate when performing a moving spiritual, a piercing hymn, or even a gospel rap. I read many stories of people being slain in the spirit at gospel concerts. Today's generation can experience some of this wonderful gospel thanks to modern social media like YouTube. I began my formal singing at St. Andrews African Methodist Episcopal Zion church as a member of the junior choir. The songs sung in the Methodist Church were a little more structured than the songs I recalled at St John and Christian Chapel.

The church has always been known as a place where the worshipers were free to get caught up in the singer or speaker's words. History has proven, clearly, for the majority of African Americans that we were greatly moved, and our spirits uplifted, by the songs of Zion. They still resonate with us today. I simply love gospel music. I am fascinated by its history. I love the stories surrounding its great performers and the trailblazing hits of the golden gospel era. I find it interesting that these performers had titles such as "Mother" Willie Mae Ford Smith, "Madame" Edna Gallmon Cooke, "Thunderbolt of the Midwest" Joe May, and many others. They even had royal titles and a hierarchy like the "Father" of gospel, Dr. Thomas Andrew Dorsey; the "King" of gospel, Rev. James Cleveland; the "Queen" of gospel, Albertina Walker; or the "First Lady" of gospel, Evangelist Shirley Caesar. The world's greatest gospel singer was unquestionably Mahalia Jackson. Aside from the cultural connection, the reflection on these great singers and their legacy helps me to recall the wonderful years of my youth and appreciate the folks who are responsible for my place in history. I use the songs we sang in church on Sunday to get me through the week. Many times, these songs were all that sustained me. One of my greatest treasures was a book call "Gospel Pearls." I also had a copy of the Baptist Hymnal. I shopped at music stores and purchased copies of The Martin and Martin Songbook and other gospel sheet music. I love to sing the hymns of the church in their original format.

There is something uplifting about the way the old anthems were sung. Likewise, I owned one of the largest gospel album collections this side of the manufacturer's shop. However, nothing could compare to the treasures contained in the "Gospel Pearls." Of all the questions I asked Grandma Ruth, I never asked her if my dad could sing. I'd like to know where I got that talent from. It's funny how I never thought about this before writing this book. Music and the arts are a new conversation topic for my dad and me. One thing is for sure—I love to sing, and I love the songs of the church more than any other kind of music. I know our family can sing because we have famous and near famous folks in our bloodline. I am sad that I do not know about the music my father liked. I often wondered if he liked music. Did it give him comfort when he was going through difficult times? ***"Dad, what is your favorite song or music style?"*** Those of us who grew up in the spirit-filled churches can relate to the question, "What happens at concerts featuring Sam Cooke and the Soul Stirrers?" Attendees literally fainted during these concerts. Much like the secular performances, gospel performers became known for their showmanship. Thus, the church has not been without its great performers in the pulpit and choir stand. I don't think we will see the likes of Clara Ward and the Famous Ward Singers of Philadelphia or some of the popular male groups of the golden gospel era repeated in the 21st century.

I recall as a child listening to the Sunday morning gospel songs on the radio and getting a feel for who were the popular singers. Then I'd go to church and hear the choirs and soloists perform the latest gospel hits. Something else striking was the preservation of the old-fashioned style of gospel singing. Today, many of the churches have set aside the songs that brought us over (as the elders would say). For me, the highlight of the day was the after-church dinners and the Sunday-night singing. As far as I was concerned, no one could sing "Precious Lord" like Cousin Lucy Bragg's son, Preston. During the civil rights movement, many of the great songs of the church were used to carry the message of the struggle for justice and equality. I find this to also be the case during the early years of African Americans down south. I look back now and wish that I could have been at a concert to see the powerful gospel singers of the day. These songs had a purpose that extended beyond the church. They gave comfort to those facing difficulties on all fronts. These songs and the comfort they gave helped many connect with the faith they needed to persevere and handle difficult situations. I know I was certainly comforted during troublesome times after leaving home to live on my own. Many of these singers encountered the same civil rights violations as the residents of the Deep South, although they were of celebrity status. I recall attending concerts in Washington, DC and listening to great gospel singers like Dr. J. Robert Bradley, Dorothy Love Coats and The Original Gospel Harmonetts, Albertina Walker and the Caravans, and others.

During one of the intermissions, I asked Dorothy Love Coats about the song she recorded, "Get Away Jordan." I felt it expressed the testimony of a faithful servant making it in and able to rest from his or her toilsome journey. Their powerful performance of that song became one of my favorites. I asked Mrs. Coats to sing that song when they went back upstairs for the second part of the program, and she replied, "We haven't done that song in years." She was pleased a young kid was fond of songs from the golden gospel era. Her group took the audience to a new level of gospel pandemonium with their performance of this song in 1955 at the Los Angeles Shrine Auditorium. While in Washington, DC, I tried to take in as many of the great concerts as possible. My church buddies, Fred, Ann, Joaquin, and I would frequent the megachurches and fill our hearts with joy in awe as these great performers delivered the message in song. I wish I could have taken in some of their live performances at the Newport Jazz festivals. Although they were of celebrity status, they were approachable. On Sundays we held our gospel service, and it was our turn to showcase our own celebrities.

The Fort Myer Gospel Choir had some of the best voices on Fort Myer, and we quickly earned a reputation for our singing ability. Tina Woods and Sandy Burrell could put any popular singer to shame. You could not sit still when they took over the mike. We sang at the Pentagon for the Black History Month programs and also went on a Southeastern United States Concert Tour. The Southeastern tour was followed by a New England Concert Tour. It was on the Southeastern tour that I met my first wife, Cathy. The Southeastern tour encompassed several major military installations from the capital region all the way down to Orlando, Florida. We slept at the military bases and sang at the military chapels. Along the way we stopped at a local church in South Carolina and in Florida at the home church of Rev. Walton. This was an extremely rewarding experience for the choir, escorts, and ushers. I sang with the choir at First AME Zion Church San Francisco and really enjoyed the majestic sound that resonated throughout the town on 1st Sunday mornings when most churches would feature their cathedral choirs. I particularly enjoyed when we would hold special concerts. Othello Jefferson was a young kid in high school when I began singing at First Church San Francisco, and I watched him mature into the wonderful minister of music and educator he is today. He accompanied me when Joyce Shepard featured me in concert on a benefit program for her Stewardess Board.

I never joined a choir when I moved to Hawaii, a decision that I truly regret. However, at my favorite place of worship, Trinity Missionary Baptist Church, I was quite fond of two of their lead singers, Normia Carter and Mickie Fine. They have powerful voices, and they always take me back to my roots when they step up to the mike. No matter what troubles the soul, music is the best medicine. I can personally attest that a song in your heart can help to overcome the worst of life's trials. Many who visit my office will quickly learn of my deep love for the music of the African American church. Listing to the songs of Zion kept me connected to my heritage. Perhaps, in retrospect, this unique music tells the story of our indigenous people. Down through the years we may have changed the tempo and phraseology, but we held true to our core heritage and, more importantly, the powerful messages they convey. This great music started long before there was a traditional African American Church. Clearly, we have been singing Zion's songs for a long time!

"A Friend in your Life"

When the four seasons of my being are coming to an end,

There in the winter of life may we look back and reflect,

Being able to call you my friend has made all the difference.

In humble adoration, shall it be said...

Somewhere between my spring rising and my winter departure,

I've been truly blessed with the great gift of your friendship.

The strength of its beauty is in its commitment.

At least two committed hearts willing to share—

Not because of birth obligation, random oath, or regulation.

Rather a pure desire to give oneself for the betterment of mankind.

Yesterday you made the decision that you would be my friend.

So how can I ever repay the great debt of love I owe—

Still, the great king with his vast wealth will not have had so great a treasure as I—

Save, he too, can call you his friend.

That day you proved your friendship when you stood by my side.

That something within you had to have been real.

For you allowed the portals of your heart to swing open wide.

Yielding an endless bounty of a caring heart unto a needing soul.

You saved me from great destruction with the power of your love.

So greater love I've come to know—simply because of you my friend.

Tomorrow will not be—unless I share with someone else the worth of its call.

Still, deep down within the bowels of my soul, my heart grows sad.

For I feel so few shall ever taste the rich nectar of true friendship.

In your presence I feel peace, I know I can trust you, I believe in you. You are my friend!

Alphonso Braggs

"The Captivating Love of the Blackberry Nectar"

Glance at any one of those Bragg men, and before you can open your mouth, you say to yourself, "He's pretty easy on the eyes." Commonly known as tall, tan, or dark, and handsome, we perpetuate a legacy of lovers with a well-known reputation for ensuring the expansion of the blackberry patch. Consequently, along this journey called life, the blackberry seed encountered an indispensable substance that we just cannot seem to live without. Yes, it is safe to say that we know a thing or two about love and relationships. Although we may have engaged in multiple relationships, we are equally and intimately familiar with the absence of love. In the end, it is that absence, experience, and diametrical understanding of the two that make us better lovers and more desirous of true love.

I, like future generations, will pause and ponder these "love" questions. Some of our modern-day practices may have stemmed from our inherited behaviors—it is in the genes. However, just because it's in the genes does not mean we can be irresponsible. So, we won't! **Dad, am I to presume that we are quite adept at getting ourselves in these love situations and then having to figure out later that we may have been better to stay with the original plan?** I think we want and work hard at being great lovers and, even more important, making sure our children know the love of their parents. I believe we want to create a foundation of relationship and family based on God's love. I often wonder how old my father was when he first fell in love and what it felt like to him. How did he know that it was really love?

I tend to base a lot of things on Grandma Ruth's example of love and the peace it exudes. I am also taken by the way a foundation of unconditional love affects the decision-making process of mature men. I would have loved to introduce my dad to the women who turned my heart upside down, broke loose the chains, and made love flow like a mighty raging river. Many have reservations when it comes to talking about the "L" word. I also believe that few men truly acknowledge falling deeply in love. I don't understand why. However, if you have ever truly been in love or witnessed firsthand its unrelenting governance over the heart, you can understand why it is not something you can easily hide or find cause to be ashamed of acknowledging. A more amazing fact is we have the ability to fall in love more than once. I believe there is a distinct difference between being in love and being with someone. Being in love requires that you start with the purest form of you! Being in love is an out-of-this-world experience with no need to fear traveling in space because you are anchored by a proven reality and trusted safety net. Figuratively and in the literal sense, it is one of the greatest things a human will ever experience. I had no idea what it would be like, but once it happened, it was game over. It was the best thing that ever happened to me. Too good to let go of and so frightening because I had no control on its length of stay or future plans. It is freer than any constitutional guarantee. As men, we tend not to embrace its stronghold because its loss is more than we care to publicly acknowledge. *"Dad, were you ever afraid of losing a love."*

My closest friends will tell you that when I fell in love for the first time as an adult, it was with a precious pearl named Marsha. The love I felt for her, some would say, was a testament to the beauty of the most memorable sunrise and sunset encapsulated in one. Simply put, she caused me to lose track of time, and so my heart was suspended in perpetual moments of grace and gratitude. I could see the sunset; yet it never disappeared. It felt like I transcended all the elements of love personified to the ninth degree. My heart spanned the essence of time and invoked a quickness that mandated she be relegated to a place of near reverence second only to God. It was easy to hold her in this special acclaim as she was one of the gentlest and naturally beautiful women I had ever seen. Loving her seemed so pure and compelling! I saw my grandfather falling in love with my grandmother every time I laid eyes on her and said to myself, *This is what it must have been like.*

How can a man ever forget the first time he fell in love? I still to this day recall the very day, time, location, and setting where my heart paused and said within, *I surrender.* Whenever I gazed upon this Godly essence of beauty and virtue, my faculties concluded, behold the "Queen." She had such a sweet and spectacular radiance about her. The foundation of my love for Marsha was based primarily on what I knew about God's love for mankind and Grandma Ruth's unconditional love. No need for Monday morning quarterbacking here! It was the real thing. I didn't plan it, but once that train started coming down the track, there was no stopping. I simply got onboard and rode it safely into town. I got onboard not really knowing where it would lead. Guided by a strong faith and a sweet reflection on that other woman I loved, Ruth, I knew there was no reason for concern. She was easy to love and whatever her imperfections (*I was too taken to acknowledge*), they were instantly made perfect by her soothing voice, humble spirit, genuine smile, and, more importantly, her love for God. Love is free. Love is liberating. Love is pure. Most of all, it is honorable and contrary to some extremely popular opinions, it never hurts. At times, it may cause you to experience the realities of life. We may experience what my Christian buddy, Mike, from the Fort Myer Gospel Service would term as "a momentary affliction." Be realistic; there will be rainy days, cloudy skies, and even thunderous nights. However, if we understand the purpose of the rain and see it for its true value, we can celebrate when the storm passes over. There are times in our lives when the night storm seems long. There are times when the clouds get dark and shield the sun. We may begin to fear the unknown. Keep in mind that the thunder is a preparation phase for what is to come. Hold fast, and just keep the faith; joy comes with the dawn of the new day. Thus, we need to embrace the confidence that comes from enduring the long restless night.

Real love has the capacity to heal our momentary afflictions and put us in a place of liberty to love even greater the next time. No matter what, there is never any shame or sorrow from being in love. **Dad, what do you make of Great-Great-Grandpa Alfred Bragg, marrying my 17-year-old Great-Great-Grandma when he was 45? Do we know if he had another family before her?** I believe human beings were created with three controlling chambers. Each chamber commands a percentage of control over our being. The upper chamber commands 30 percent. The middle chamber commands 40 percent. The bottom chamber commands the final 30 percent. Our ability to genuinely love and receive love is based on the control we yield from these chambers. Optimizing the degree of control and reciprocation from these chambers is what makes love a beautiful and most powerful experience. The irony is that some only want one or more chambers but hesitate to take the full set because it *obligates them to the more noble purpose of the Creator.*

Given that the heart is located in the middle chamber, victory is guaranteed when the upper or lower chamber unites with the middle chamber. This is true because of the immutable law of unconditional love. In a perfect scenario, all three chambers are on one accord and we have as perfect a *"love"* as mankind will ever experience. Sometimes the chambers are at odds over the priorities of love, and the result is either a physical gratification and compromise or a reaffirmation of the power of spiritual convictions. If we allow ourselves to get caught up and yield the security and control of our chambers for the wrong purpose, we eventually lose out. There are those who would try to persuade us to override the middle chamber by uniting the upper and lower chambers. The end result is called bitter fruit. Bitter fruit must not be allowed to grow in the blackberry patch. Its foul seeds will rob the tender buds of their God-given fragrances and succulent delights. While we can never ensure that all fruit will be healthy fruit, a vigilant caretaker will prune the patch to ensure the best harvest. Therefore, the Bragg blackberry patch will perpetuate a legacy that helps them to make healthy choices and ensure the safety and security of our sacred chambers of love. The late jazz singer Dinah Washington had a popular song that I truly love entitled "This Bitter Earth." I would sing this song over and over. It was such a powerful proclamation of valuing and allowing an acknowledgment of devaluing our self-love and what we should expect when it comes to love and relationships.

"This Bitter Earth"
This bitter earth what fruit it bears.
What good is love that no one shares?
And if my life is like the dust that hides the glow of a rose.
What good am I, Heaven only knows.
This bitter earth can it be so cold?
Today you are young, too soon you're old
But while a voice within me cries.
I'm sure someone may answer my call.
And this bitter earth may not be so bitter after all
Lyrics by Dinah Washington

I think there are several phases to giving and receiving this blackberry seed's love. The first and most important is realizing the Creator is the main source of true love. For those that are not of a faith or conviction, I have no explanation. Find that eternal source and make it your number one. Second, when we accept the Creator's love, it should compel us to love ourselves without conditions. The Creator's love makes us accountable to ourselves and to the Creator. Third, we should feel obligated to share the Creator's love with those around us who we have been blessed to share this journey called life. A fourth phase is loving such that the produce from the blackberry vine will continue to perpetuate this legacy of love to future generations, and the legacy of loving the blackberry seed lives on into infamy. How blessed is the man or woman who comes into the fold of love and learns the difference between the real and the perception. Blessed also is the man or woman who endures life's tragedies and eventually crosses the path of love. Every day of my life I thank Grandma Ruth for teaching me that one day a young lady would come along like Marsha and I would know that God has found enough favor in me that I may share with her what He has been sharing with me all these years. Do not call me sacrilegious. I am simply suggesting that passing on this blackberry seed is merely passing on God's natural fruit to those we engage with to create future generations. Those who enjoy fresh fruit from the vine will realize and appreciate the maturity of this blackberry seed nectar and ultimately experience the bounty of God's love.

Love is an amazing thing. It can be enjoyed from afar, or we can boldly experience it fresh from the vine. Many people are reluctant to embrace real love because of their situations. Consequently, those in need of having real love passed on are neglected and the Creator's reciprocal process of perpetual love is interrupted. This scenario is most unfortunate, but all too true for many of today's generations. In life I think that we have choices when it comes to love. We can wallow in the sadness of its absence or hold firm in our faith that should all else fail, God loves us. His love is so great that we can literally experience it and understand how and what comprises love. When we make that our base, it is easier to acknowledge the second important aspect of finding love: the significance of loving ourselves. It is easy to love ourselves once we recognize our own great sense of worth.

We move on from there to a philosophy of sharing love. We exercise the same principle that God uses—to love despite being loved. Keeping the faith, we find that we are loved in return. The truth be told, I have always been loved. We just never fully acknowledge how much and by whom. It is only when we take the time to allow ourselves to be loved that we discover just how much love we have to give and received. As we live and grow, we continue to find love. Man, what a blessing. One young lady at Holy Light Church caught my attention in an incredibly special way. Her name was Janice, and she was a bundle of sweetness and purity. She was committed in her pursuit of eternal life and never allowed herself to be distracted. Janice lived not too far from Rev. Vaughn. Janice's grandmother lived right across the street from Rev. Vaughn. I was particularly drawn to her grandmother because she reminded me so much of my Grandma Ruth. It goes without saying that Janice had my heart. I guess I tried to get back into a relationship too soon after breaking up with Marsha. Although Marsha and I never became husband and wife, we accomplished a higher calling of two people knowing what true love is and how we can have it for the rest of our lives. As my friends would subsequently declare, I defined true love by how I felt for Marsha. Moreover, I know now what it should be like and how to confirm its realness. Our Pastor at the Fort Myer Gospel Service, Rev. Walton, had a cousin in Sanford, Florida. He told us before we went on the Southeastern Gospel Concert Tour that someone was going to *"get caught down there."* Sure enough, it happened to me. I was blessed to meet his cousin Cathy Ann when we stopped at his home church to do a concert. She was young, pure, and devout. It did not take long to realize that she had all the qualities a man was looking for in a wife and mother for his children. Within a year of meeting, I was at the altar saying, "I do!" It was almost unbelievable.

Cathy was a virtuous woman. She came from a devoutly strong Christian family, and you could not help but fall in love the first time you met them. I knew Gene and Carrie but never gave thought to the fact that all of his extended family were as loving and kind. Although it may seem irrelevant, she came from a family skilled in the fine art of southern cuisine preparation. Quite frankly, it was important to me that my wife knew how to cook. When we went to her hometown for the concert, her family prepared food for the choir. How ironic that the one food item I was most pleased with and made the biggest fuss over came from her mother's kitchen. Most men are reluctant to look back and say they made a mistake by letting a "good one" get away. I raise this point to acknowledge that few men will ever be as blessed as I was to have had such a wonderful being as Cathy commit herself to them for life. Gosh, if only we could look down the road and then decide if we are doing the right thing! I keep saying it over and over—I am a very, very blessed man!

When Cathy and I made plans to marry, we knew to expect a large attendance. A big group from the Fort Myer Gospel Service rented cars, and we drove down to Florida for the wedding. Because Grandma Rosabell was not able to travel to Florida, we held a separate wedding reception in North Carolina at my home church, St. Andrew, and everyone gave us such an outpouring of love. When I returned to work at the Pentagon, the office staff gave me a warm and generous reception. I was most surprised by the kindness of the janitorial staff who called me in on their break one afternoon to have a little reception and gift presentation. I was truly overwhelmed. Falling in love is one thing. But what is love if there are no friends and family to share that joyous experience? I felt overly blessed as all of our friends and family gave tremendously to this union. At every turn, we were showered with love time after time. I had only a few months left on my tour at the Pentagon when I married. While waiting to move to my next duty station, we shared a big house with my friend Ann in Silver Spring, Maryland. Soon, I was on my way to Groton, Connecticut for submarine duty and Cathy was about to experience the perils of being a Navy wife. A second and equally important lesson is fostering a respectful and healthy relationship after you transition as a couple. Note these irreplaceable words: "respectful" and "healthy." It is not the number of times you fall in love, but the sincerity of the heart that allows you to transition relationships in a healthy manner. Therefore, we are able to experience genuine love time after time as we move from one relationship to another. This is not to encourage change. Rather, should you change, do not change the values that make a relationship healthy.

A few years after transferring to California with the Navy, I became smitten by a beautiful California girl named Patricia Ann. Yes, it is true that California girls are "hot," and yes, you want to get to know them better. Regardless of where you live, most men will agree that there are two primary places to meet women: church and clubs. I met the future mother of my children in the church. I have done pretty well at church. At Patricia and I's wedding, I sang a song I wrote several years earlier while I was in Connecticut. We were married in the lovely California country and within a year moved to beautiful Hawaii with the family. I will always be grateful to her for blessing me with a family to come home to and supporting me in my naval career. It is not an easy job being married to a Fast Attack Submarine Sailor. They have a very demanding schedule and are constantly on the go. She was a mainstay for the kids, and no man can ever ask for more, especially when we are always gone away from home. Loving and receiving love from the blackberry seed is a good thing. In fact, it is a blessing from God. None of us are perfect. Instead, our love is made perfect by holding firm to our faith in God. Over the years, I encountered a few more special blessings of love while living in Hawaii. The blackberry patch has made it down through the years because of a firm belief in a true and living God.

Our ability to love and be loved can never be taken for granted. It is my prayer that my children will want their children to know the stories of our love experiences. Moreover, I pray that the truth of these stories will empower them to embrace love and never be afraid to love. When it comes to the blessings of love, I reflect on the legacy of my blackberry seed. I think about the moment that I wanted to present my children to my beloved grandmothers, and they were resting in Heaven. However, my maternal Great-Grandmother Hattie Nixon was alive when Andre was born. I thought it appropriate that I should present him to her as a token of my commitment to this precious blackberry patch. Andre may never recall meeting his Great-Great-Grandma Hattie, but that historic moment will live on as one of the proudest days in my life. When it comes to motherhood and sisterhood, our blackberry seed legacy fosters a philosophy of respect for the women in our lives. All too often, we fail to adequately recognize them. After all, none of us would be here today were it not for those women laboring in pain just so that we could exist. Therefore, I will always hold them in high regard.

A lot has been said about the Bragg men and our philosophy on love. Most of those stories centered on us having multiple families. Regardless, I am proud to say that the majority of us have been responsible. Where we have not been responsible, God has filled the void, and we still can shout the victory for our children's sake. I think it's because of the fervent prayers of faithful women like Grandma Ruth nurturing blackberry seeds. I am proud to know that I am not the only Bragg who feels this way and take comfort in knowing that the future looks good for loving the bearers of strong blackberry seeds.

"Growing Friendship Vines"

Growing up, I can't really say I had friends in the true sense of the word. I had playmates at school and kids in the neighborhood who hung out with us. At school, there were some kids I felt closer to than others, primarily based on activities such as church, organizations, and events. It was not until I was away from home and serving in the military that I was able to truly define and experience the real meaning of friendship. There are as many definitions of friends as there are people who will give you their opinion. Nowhere else is this more prevalent than in the military. I found that in the Navy, we tend to have a lot of associates. I submit that there is a great confusion between a coworker, associate, acquaintance, and friend. I believe that we place a person in a particular category based on what we want out of a certain type of relationship. It is also based on what we bring to the relationship. I live with a firm conviction that once a declaration of friendship has been made, it is for life. Friendship is a rare privilege that someone bestows upon us, and I feel that too many people take the bestowal for granted. Friendship is the highest association two or more people can have between each other not regulated by law or obligated by biology. It is understandable why people associated by marriage or blood are close. However, a greater commitment of closeness is demonstrated when there is a declaration of friendship.

Even today, I cannot say that I have a lot of friends. Honestly, I never wanted a lot of friends. I do admit that I deeply care for and have close association with a lot of people. I was grown before I had my first real friend. I entered this association with some predispositions about what friendship should be and how I would differentiate between those in the category of associates, acquaintances, coworkers, and friends. I knew from the beginning that my friends would be of great significance, and therefore I would reserve my friendship for the selected few. Although I attribute the majority of my friendships to associations made during my naval career, they are not solely based on the traditional "military comradely." While stationed at the Pentagon, I was blessed to have four persons bestow upon me the honor of their friendship. Subsequently, we have been friends for life. Victor Blair, Bruce James, Fred Clark, and Marsha Johnson forged a special relationship that has weathered the changing storms of time. This bond has expanded as our families have grown. Each became my friend through different situations. However, we all shared that one common fortune of giving of ourselves to one another. No matter how long we may have been apart, it is like we were never apart when we got the chance to see each other. Victor became my first best friend. Looking back, I would have chosen no other to be there for me through all my good and bad times. It began shortly after I arrived at Fort Myer. I met Victor during a game of pool at the recreation center. In those days, we played a lot of pool, Ping-Pong, cards, Pac-Man, chess, and checkers.

Victor took time with me to teach me what he knew and could always be counted on for a fair game of pool. He taught me everything I know. Turns out, he was going through boot camp in a different company and remembered seeing me. I was not the most outgoing guy on post and tended to hang out at the recreation center or at the lounge. Another group of guys also liked to hang out a lot in those same places, and Victor was in that group. I soon had someone that I could go places with and do different things with. Victor was good for morale. He was always upbeat and was never without his "unique" smile. We lived in the same building, and he was the first person brave enough to try to teach me to swim. We served as best man for each other's weddings. I got to know his family, and several years later, I married a young lady from his neck of the woods. Victor didn't stay in the Navy and returned to his home in Florida after a few years in the Washington, DC area. The day he left was one of the saddest days in my naval career. I went back to my room and literally wept. My best friend had gone back home.

Victor was always there for me. There were times he did not even know the difference he was making in my life. He was a true confidant and trusted friend. As we advanced in rank, Victor purchased a car. I didn't know how to drive, so I took driving lessons. A true testament of our friendship was Victor allowing me to drive his car. It was a neat little white Monte Carlo with a blue top. It was something to have a car in those days and be able to go off base when you needed or wanted. One day, I had the car and was leaving the parking lot when Victor flagged me down. I put the car in reverse and started backing down the street to where he was standing. Nervous and not all that comfortable driving in reverse with a lot of folks watching, I ran the whitewalls up against the curb. I was so embarrassed. My friend chastised me, but still allowed me to drive the car. I had gotten back in church by the time Victor was due to leave the Navy. Being a renewed convert to Christ, I could think of no one that I wanted to also convert more than my best friend Victor. The reaffirmation of my religious beliefs also helped me better understand what friendship was also about. It made me be real with those I called my friends. I was so pleased that Victor went to church with me a few times before he left to go home to Florida. The night before Victor left, I reminded him to stop by my room before leaving since I had a gift for him. I purchased a bible for him and had his name inscribed on the front cover. I gave him a little card that told him how much I appreciated our friendship. I told him I wished I could give him a bigger gift, but the biggest gift had already been given when God gave us His son Jesus. I told him I wanted him to know God as I did, and I didn't want him to miss out. I recall saying while timing is important, he did not have to accept Christ until he was ready. I could see his heart was moved. Emotionally taken, he went to the restroom to gather himself and then returned. With his ever-present captivating smile, he said he was ready to make that journey back to Florida.

Reflecting back on the moment, I knew he was doing what he does best—being strong for others. We talked about keeping in touch and his plans after the Navy. We made some promises to each other. Then I walked my friend out to the parking lot and watched him drive off. I did not know what the future held, but my faith told me this was not our last exchange. I think that is the day that I knew for sure that we were lifetime friends. His departure was also a good thing, because it taught me that you could still experience true friendship from afar. God knew the impact that his departure had on me and saw to it that as a young Christian, I had friends. The church gave me my next set of friends. I met a young man at the Fort Myer Gospel Service name Bruce James. Bruce was a member of the 3rd Infantry, The Old Guard. He was a genuinely good person with a polite and calm disposition. We visited each other's barracks and went to church and bible study together. He was my primary access to the Army folks and taught me a good deal about soldiers.

While I did not plan it that way, I began making a lot of friends from Florida Bruce's best buddy was Darnell Strick, and we enjoyed hanging out on our free weekends. All of us came from religious families so we appreciated good preaching and singing. We visited numerous churches around the Washington, DC area. ne of our favorite delights was gospel concerts. I think we covered all the big-name gospel singers who came to the nation's capital area. At a minimum, we made sure at least one of us had tickets. Whenever one of us did not attend, we made sure we shared the highlights from the concert, and especially information on any new songs. When Bruce got married, instead of losing a friend I gained a friend's family. Vera was a welcomed addition to the fold. Soon the family began to grow, and there were two little girls, Crystal and Stacy. We were blessed to use Bruce and Vera's home for the weekends. We had a place to go and get home-cooked meals. Mostly it meant we could leave the base, and it was within walking distance. The commissary was on the way to the house, so everything was convenient. Looking back, it is amazing how much walking we all did and never complained or felt as though we didn't have enough to enjoy life. We were young so we did not have an appreciation for how we may be invading the young couple's space. This was a lesson we had to learn, and because we were friends, it was a lesson we respected. Bruce became my closest confidant when Victor left the area. He had an inviting spirit. Still, he was the kind of young man who made you feel as though you never wanted to disappoint or cross him—the kind of brother everyone yearned to have as a friend. He was protective, fair, caring, and firm.

He made sure he checked in on you if you missed church or he didn't see you for a while. A lot of us learned what it was to be a good Christian, husband, and father by his personal example. Loyalty is another one of his major qualities. Not everyone was kind to me; on more than one occasion Bruce stood up for me. He took care of his friends. Bruce had a way of being straight up about things. He had a physical presence that could be intimidating if you did not know him. However, it was hard for you to get upset with him because he was so caring. You always knew where you stood with him, and, above everything else, he treated everyone with respect. I will never forget Bruce's visit shortly after Marsha and I broke up. More than anyone else, he knew how much I loved Marsha. He would be the first one to say I had a petition going to get Webster to add a new example to the definition of love, *"Alphonso's love for Marsha."* He proved a great comfort and assisted tremendously in helping me to stay grounded mentally and spiritually. My time in the nation's capital was a wonderful time. Bruce had a lot to do with me enjoying my time at the seat of government. I met a lot of soldiers through knowing Bruce. Fred Clark was one such soldier.

Fred Clark performed an administrative job in the Army, whereas Bruce was an infantryman. He had a desk job, so I could better relate to his profession. I enjoyed discussing the parallel of my job and his with our other buddies. Fred was older and a seasoned military man. Fred lived in my building and joined our Fort Myer Gospel Service. He also had a car, a great asset. Real friends enjoy each other's company and are able to go places and do exciting things and not worry about things. We genuinely trusted each other. I will never forget the summer vacations we took together. We drove from Washington, DC to Florida and back. It was a great time. We stopped at every amusement park along the way and visited his family in Georgia. Brother Fred, as we affectionately called him, could be relied upon to always be there. Sometimes we would skip out on our regular church service and visit some of the churches in Washington, DC Although it was not a routine practice, we could always be found at the Springfield Baptist Church listening to Pastor L. R. Jones. On those Sunday's when we did not have big fellowships, Fred and I would go over to Washington, DC to one of our favorite soul food restaurants on Georgia Avenue near Howard University. Later we would drive around the district and enjoy the beautiful Sunday afternoon park scenes.

Fred has always been a great confidant. We could talk to each other about anything, and he proved to be a great source of strength. Our conversations would routinely begin with formal salutations: *"Hello, Mr. Braggs"* and *"Yes, Mr. Clark"* were always the order of the day for us. One of the things I like most about Fred is his love of the old-style gospel music. We would spend countless hours shopping for or listening to the old-time gospel singers. We would not dare miss the opportunity to catch a concert featuring some of the legends. We were barely able to contain ourselves when he got to see Dr. J. Robert Bradley in concert. It was never a matter the time of day or situation; Fred has always been there for his friends. As I transitioned from the nation's capital to New England, I made new friends. Most of them were affiliated with the church we attended. A few were from the ship. One of the most respected friendships onboard the USS George C. Marshall Submarine was John Wesley Warren Jr. from the Charleston, South Carolina area.
John took great care of me when I reported to the ship, and his wife Marchelle was also there for my wife Cathy as we tried to get settled in Groton, Connecticut. Our wives became great friends. I was proud to see John move on in his career and had the honor of witnessing him advance to the rank of Senior Chief Petty Officer, U.S. Navy.

When I transferred from the East Coast to the West Coast, I felt alone again and truly separated from my close friends. However, it did not take long to establish some great friendships onboard USS Hawkbill, USS Los Angeles, Submarine Force Pacific Headquarters, and USS Honolulu. Zebedee Rivera and Johnathan Miles were both shipmates and trusted roommates. I could talk to Zebedee about anything, and we visited regularly on the USS Hawkbill Submarine. Zebedee had boundless energy, and he illuminated the room wherever he was. He had a strong appreciation for cultural values, and he invoked those around him to do the same. He was a very creative mind and shared with us his talents in poetry and paintings. I am deeply honored to have some of them in my home today. Johnathan was an ambitious young fella from Texas with big and bold plans. He never stopped dreaming or challenging others to dream or pursue their goals. He was lively and kept the party going when in a crowd. At home, he was just a regular guy who could hold deep conversations and debate the hot topics of the day. He always pushed me to be better tomorrow than I was today. I am always in awe of his ability to excel in any endeavor. During our time together, I got to know their families and was made to feel like we were old friends. Zebedee was someone I could not only trust but spend countless hours just sitting and talking with. He always made sure there was value added to each engagement. I will always treasure the relationships I made with Clinton Burr, Norman Lloyd, Travis Hunt, Bart Tramer, Otha Livingston, Christopher Druesedow, John Curren, and so many others.

My young ones (as I like to refer to them) always kept me on my toes. Some like Druesedow had a drive to excel that should have been in the Indy 500. Their drive paid off, and I am equally proud of their successful careers outside of the Navy. Yes, I was enormously proud to take ownership of that special trust they allowed. David Jiménez, Shawn Frison, Ray Wall, Gary Thornton, and others were not in my division, but we forged lasting friendships. Jiménez could always be found in my office after watch. He visited after he changed commands and stayed in touch. Like the rest, I was proud to witness their ascent up the ladder of success. All found numerous ways to make me know that my life had purpose for our paths crossing. As people moved around, they continued to share well after settling down in their personal lives as parents and business owners. It's special when I spend time with their kids and talk about the days their dads were in the Navy. As much as I cared for them, they cared for me, and it showed frequently. I will never forget the time I pulled a chest muscle lifting a large printer in the ship's office. At the time, it did not hurt. However, by the time I got home that evening, I was in great distress. I called back down to the ship and Travis answered the phone. I told him clearly not to make a deal of it or tell anyone but have the corpsman come check on me because I was having pains in my chest.

He informed everyone in the duty section, and I was embarrassed but grateful for him caring. That is one story that they will never let me forget. I did not usually pull pranks, but I finally got Travis back when I found a creative way to inform him that he had been selected for promotion. Norman and Otha were like fighting brothers I constantly had to split up. Still, they would not allow anyone to talk about the other. I think I saved Norman's life once or twice, but that's another story that we all laugh about when we gather and tell sea stories. I would leave Otha in charge of things, but Norman would act like he was running the show. I could always count on their parents' help when they got too out of hand. That is another story that only Norman likes to share, and then we laugh for hours. I have fond memories of watching movies in the ship's office on Saturday nights for my very own Francklyn Celestin and his two besties, Von Johnson and Frangeone Delouis. These three bonded long before we served, and it's been a memorable journey since. I tend to think that I taught Jason Tapia and Johnathan Miles a thing or two about cribbage. Executive and Supply guys were pretty close. Wonderful friends like Jason DeGraff, Bobby Brown, and Chuck Morton never forgot about my special diet needs. They were even nice enough to sneak me a fresh baked cookie or two during those all-night watches on deployment.

Included in the many underway highlights were special meals we would prepare for the crew such as during Black History Month or Chief's pizza night. I watched them grow up to become mature young men, and they watched me become a wise old man *("Ole Smoothie"* as DeGraff would say). I was like a big brother and father figure to many throughout my Navy career. he ship's office became the gathering place. In my naval career I was blessed to have a special bond that only exists among a band of brothers in the Chief Petty Officers' Mess. Even in retirement, I enjoyed the bonds of brotherhood with the best in the mess like Phil Bissainthe. They don't make them any better than William "Billy" Cramer and Gamal Coles. They were dear friends and true fraternal brothers. The crew loved them; all you had to do was spend a little time with them, and it was clear why they were so adored. Every chief had a running mate, and I had my favorite in Mike Jones. We just seemed to click, and it really helped to have a brother in the mess that you could talk to about things at the mess level. We had the benefit of our wives being good friends, and we really enjoyed the weekend fellowships.

After retiring from the military, I found a new group to establish close relationships with through my professional association in the National Association for the Advancement of Colored People (NAACP), Prince Hall Masons and Shriners, Blacks In Government, and Alpha Phi Alpha Fraternity, Inc. Likewise, I am blessed to again kindle the bonds that exist between shipmates as a federal employee working with the Department of the Navy. Few can say they have the privilege of knowing so many strong brothers who they can truly depend on when in need. I must admit, though, that these brothers don't play! Although we love to laugh and joke, we are still men of character! I like how we hold each other accountable. Willie Agee, James Brown, Howard Covington, Jay Galbreath, Iverson Jarrell, Linwood Richardson, and Edward Whitehead are solid men who have made a tremendous contribution to our fraternal orders and continue to find opportunities to forge new successes.

Some of the relationships forged while I was on active duty remain strong to this date. My dear friend Jewel McDonald and I met when her acting group performed for my military group on Pearl Harbor during the late 1990s. I met Carolyn Floyd-Johnson and Tim Bolden in 1998. We have been friends since that time. Carolyn Floyd-Johnson encouraged me to be active in the local NAACP, and Tim kept me going in the community. Alexis and Vickie Carr extended a warm greeting and invited me as family into their home. My ride or die Gene Hicks has been my lifelong friend. Thanks, Flo Moore, for introducing us. These civic organizations provided me with lasting friendships.

My NAACP running mates, Anita Motte, Yolanda Johnson, Kimberly Alston, Richard Robinson, Mel Colquitt, and Rubina Collier, could always be counted on to keep me in line. Quite honestly, I would be lost without them, and I think they share the same sentiments. We fuss like battling siblings but will not let anything keep us from our determined mission. Perhaps one of the best benefits of having friends is realizing that age is not always a factor when it comes to healthy relationships. Some of the most endearing friendships are forged in the workplace. For those who are both coworkers and fraternally related, it becomes a double blessing. Along the way, I was blessed with great mentorship by the likes of Ed Young, Judge Sandra Simms, and Faye Kennedy.

As I write this book and especially this section, I now find myself asking whether other mature adults have young friends, as I do and have been blessed by over these past decades. There is not a turn in the day where I am not met with the humbling greeting of caring young men and women who afford me the opportunity to call them friend. Some have given me a more distinct honor of being their mentor, and I truly look forward to my regular sessions with them all. I must admit that mentees Khyri Baker, Kimathi Clark, Willie Clark, Tito Garcia, Nic Graham, Richard Jeanpierre, James Nunnelly, Shawn Ricks, DeDaryl Stringfield, John Watkins, Ray Williams, and so many others have done a great job at validating the highest tenants of friendship. Each season blesses me with a new set of mentees and opportunities.

I feel richly blessed and highly favored to know that I can call up Stevie King, Carlos Marroquin, Josue Reyes, Joseph Summers, Michael Washington, and so many other good brothers I call friend to help out in the community. They have always placed their love of the fraternity above selfish gain, and in doing so they gained immeasurable respect and admiration. These relationships and memories continue to bring me joy. I will never forget when the Sir Knights turned out in full form to serve as ushers for Sir Knight Nick and Angel Bonds Wedding at Ala Moana Beach Park.

Nick and I became Sir Knights together, and we were never able to get through a meeting in any of our fraternal houses without laughing at each other. Of course, Nick was not alone in his mischief. He had a good partner in crime, Andre "Boogie" Thomas, to help him as they would trade off comic feats during lodge and temple meetings. What good man did not enjoy time spent fellowshipping with Edward Whitehead or enjoying special times and food at the home of Sir Knight "Big Bruiser" Brown?

The NAACP, Masons, and Greek organizations are now an integral part of my weekly engagement. Nothing compares to the wonderful fellowships we have after meetings or events as we share about our beloved organizations. The time just fades like the sunset, and before you know it, hours have passed. These are the moments that solidify our friendships and affirm our fraternal bonds. The real affirmation of these friendships is the lack of hesitation to reach out to each other regardless of the time we may have been apart. As old friendships transition on and new ones are forged, we always make sure we gather for the annual Dr. Martin Luther King Jr. Parade and Rally and the annual Juneteenth Celebration.

These are the two primary events that bring together the African American community in Hawaii. It is a great time to sit and reflect and share on what has happened since we last met. Some of those stories will stay only among true friends. Others, we will laugh at the memories like wearing mix-matched shoes to a lodge meeting and being the only one who didn't notice it until the end of the meeting. Perhaps it was that time someone wet their pants or the "eye" thing that only some of us knew about. Those may have been isolated moments. Still, they are priceless memories that last a lifetime among friends.

"What made us friends has kept us friends." That's what it means to have a friend in your life. It may sound simple, but it is a true statement. I am confident that we will continue to enjoy each other's company until God calls us home. Cemented by God's love and grace we are simply good men who became brothers for life.

"A Good Man Made Better"

I have many honors. However, the honor of being a Prince Hall Mason is among the most treasured. Founded in 1775, Prince Hall Freemasonry is one of the oldest African American professional organizations and serves as a beacon of light in the community. We are good men made better through the application of knowledge that comes from studying and applying the principles of appropriate living found in the Holy Scriptures. Freemasonry is a fraternal order of men unconditionally committed to building a better society for all of humanity, especially the less fortunate. The active part of building is found in the life we live perfecting our craft. The word "craft" refers to several facets of our order. As men of faith our craft refers to how we live as brothers, husbands, fathers, coworkers, neighbors, and citizens. We strive to improve ourselves and, thus, we improve society.

When we say we are perfecting our craft, we are speaking of perfecting the life we live through our individual and collective service to God, our neighbor, and ourselves. Among the biblical foundations we ascribe to is the story of Ruth. How ironic is it that the biblical Ruth and my beloved grandmother are profound examples for my life and legacy? Her example of selfless love and commitment to others is reflective of the love and commitment that should be exhibited by those in the fraternity.
In life we go through various stages of living. The same is true for freemasonry as we ascend from one "degree" to a higher "degree" of commitment and enlightenment. As we grow in knowledge and understanding, we are better equipped to increase our commitment, thereby perfecting our craft and improving our lives and the lives of those around us.

Prince Hall Masons embody the tenants of Friendship, Morality, and Brotherly love. Our legacy of faithful service is deeply woven in America's rich and diverse culture. The success of numerous community projects is due in part to our tireless commitment to build and sustain local communities. A technical analysis of the ancient ruins or the great pyramids bears witness to how well our ancient brothers perfected their craft and passed that legacy on to future generations. For centuries, these perfect works have endured manmade and natural disasters. As masons, we are equally obligated to have our lives represent spiritual monuments of perfection that withstand the sandstorms of time. In life there is a parallel between our works and our words. The things we do and say are the primary factors that determine our success and the success of those with whom we are entrusted to lead. Our works and our words should be emblematically anchored by a plumb. The plumb is a simple tool affixed to the end of a line or cord and when effectively used produces absolute perfection. Thus, we are reminded of the symbolic purpose and intellectual value of properly affixing a plumb to our work and words.

We are taught emblematically that our actions should be governed by the plumb. A properly affixed plumb will allow a good man to walk upright before God and man, thereby leaving a legacy befitting our august fraternity. Spiritually, we dismiss the purpose and value of the plumb when we deviate from the principles set forth by the Creator. Without the plumb, we are ill positioned to achieve and thus unable to reach that singular point of perfection required of those working in the craft.

It is also important to understand that it is not *we* that make the determination if *we* have achieved a perfect work; rather, it is **He** who has the power and authority to judge our final works and words. Accordingly, it is **He** and **He** alone that grants the ultimate reward for a life fully committed to building a better society. Upon reflection, we consider the example of Enoch and his humble lesson of being found worthy of God's reward for faithful service. As Freemasons, we are endowed with the requisite wisdom and leadership to set us on a course of achieving nobler deeds and reaching higher heights.

Wherever and whenever we assemble, our biggest challenge is to find that singular point that unites us to achieve our intended common purpose. We should therefore dedicate our efforts to uplifting humanity, strengthening society, and building better bands of brothers. We must always apply the plumb principle in our public and private lives that we may be made better for the Builder's use, that Builder being God, the Great Architect of the Universe.

Freemasons are known for their skills at building things. Symbolically, building a lodge of brothers is like building a house. The craftsman begins by laying the groundwork with four square corners resting on a solid foundation, paying careful attention to precise measurements and dimensions. The building is built with the intention of longevity, safety, security, and usefulness. The same holds true for our Masonic legacy that each brother must build. Consider the great pyramids of Egypt. The skilled craftsmen carefully measured and laid each brick according to the master builder's plan, and today we look upon them as great works. Therefore, a house built without square corners or an unleveled floor will not last; it is hazardous to its occupants and may result in the revocation of the builder's license to work in that field of labor.

Building a lodge of brothers begins with a single point and expands outward, uniting all who come in contact with its perfect purpose. Because its foundation is of a Divine construct, we are all united around its providence, thereby allowing for a harmonious gathering. Theoretically, we believe that brotherhood begins in the heart of man and extends toward his fellowman. As Freemasons, we need to periodically check the connectivity and viability of our plumb and reaffirm our commitment to this great and noble concept. Imagine what historians would say about the great pyramids if the builders had not taken care to ensure they were built with precise measurements and attention to detail. Our ancient brothers understood the value of having the right man equipped with the proper tools performing the designated task.

The same principle applies to how we should select, equip, and task brothers today. The lesson we learned is that the builders of the great pyramids used proven points and specialized tools. When our works unite, our words inspire, the builder is rewarded, and the entire brotherhood is motivated by this labor of love. The pyramids were able to be built because the young apprentice learned from the old master and experience was treasured and respected. Each of the craftsmen understood the relevance of instruments working in concert with one another. Our leadership challenge is to make sure we do not allow popularity or personality to usurp Divine providence.

Civic-minded men have a moral and ethical responsibility to contribute to the betterment of humanity. While some men are blessed with the capacity to make notable contributions, I believe the ability and degree of these contributions are based on a man's willingness to fully accept his duty to God, his family, and his fellowman. I challenge us to study the scriptures and learn from the stories of those anointed and chosen leaders of men.

For example, let us examine why Aaron was anointed and why he was chosen for his position of leadership. As Freemasons, we should humbly position ourselves to receive God's anointing and blessing of the symbolic morning dew. You have heard it said, "one band, one sound." There is a distinct difference between music and noise. Where there is harmony, there is good music.

It has been said that something is different about being in the presence of a mason. In addition to being great managers of time and disciplines, we have learned the fine art of controlling our actions by the application of Divine principles found in the Holy Writings. In this modern day, it is imperative that our legacy not be singularly defined by our impromptu action or reactions. Recognizing that our actions are an ever-present component of everyday existence, managing the impact it can have on ourselves and others is key to a healthy outcome. Masons strive to live a life well spent of purpose and honor. In the end, we pray that our white apron is as pure and spotless as the day it was conferred upon us.

These blackberry seeds initiated into this honored fraternity will confirm that we have the ability to exude emotions of positive and negative behaviors. It is not uncommon to encounter challenging ills of society that create unhealthy emotions. On any given Monday morning, we can express frustration, anger, grief, pain, hurt, excitement, and many more. These emotions can become the foundation or initiator of our poor choices. They feed vices and superfluities. This is especially true in cases of spontaneous responses. In shame, we try to hide our internal emotions that drive ill outcomes. However, hiding them does not mean they do not exist or that they have gone away.

The beauty of a healthy blackberry patch is brotherhood committed to our wellness for life. In masonry, we have a lifeline called a cable tow. In our human moments, we are pressed to answer the prevailing question: Are we adhering to the principles that reflect a purpose-driven life? Thus, it is important to take the time to quietly listen and calculate our responses. Hence, this is the primary reason why we must be governed by the plumb. Not just any plumb, but the one that allows us to walk upright as men and masons. The plumb that allows us to perpetuate a legacy of honor and integrity. The plumb that allows us to properly represent. By "represent" I mean to "re-present." Thus, we are called to re-present to future generations the tenants of our profession.

For masons, our actions must affirm we were made better. As enlightened men, our perfectly squared actions provide an excellent example on how to deal with life's vices and superfluities. The successful application of which positions us to proactively mitigate potential reactions that may impair our blackberry seed harvest. As masons, we must govern from a position of our best self. Our rich legacy teaches us to lead from the front. We are taught to be proactive. We are given the tools and supportive resources so that we can properly discern what constitutes the best the environment to work, recreate, and live in. We frequently incorporate the tenants of love, unconditional love, in our forward movements, commonly referred to as "paying it forward."

Quite honestly, the measured and responsible control we exude is based on our ability to approach situations from a position of truth, respect, and trust. At the end of the day, we keep ourselves accountable for the choices we make and how they impact our fellowman. We are ever conscious of the irreparable harm unhealthy actions can have on those we are charged to hold dear in and outside this blackberry patch. Regardless of the time of day, the beauty and essence of a well-governed blackberry seed patch can be seen from afar. Blackberry seeds selected to carry the rank and title of a mason possess the strength to stand upright at all times because they stand on a foundation of morality, ethics, and integrity. We have been blessed by a full complement of the Great Architect's working tools.

These blackberry seeds are nourished and developed to their full potential by the late-night gravitational pull of the moon, the refreshment of the morning dew, and warmth of the high noon sun. Now we patiently await the presentation, examination, and judgment of our harvest by the Judge Supreme. Finally, let us reflect on the fact that the Egyptians built huge stone tombs for ancient royalty with a square base and triangular walls that sloped at the perfect angle to end at a precise point. It took hundreds of hours and men working in concert with each other to erect these monuments of perpetual honor and distinction. As good men made better and called to *"re-present"* our beloved fraternal order, we are called to no less a noble purpose.

We are to immerse ourselves in understanding the omnipotence of the Great Architect who formed the four corners of creation from a singular point of existence to a reality of time and eternity. Therefore, let us assemble in perfect form to serve as living instruments of honor. Let us serve with distinction to proudly perpetuate our Masonic legacy. The proper application of our spiritual plumb transforms good works into great works capable of weathering the moral and intellectual challenges of perfecting our craft. This symbolic construct reveals the true beauty of holiness and affirms that our buildings are simply good men made better striving for the building not made by the hands of man, eternal in the heavens.

"There Goes an Alpha Man"

As an Alpha man, I continue a proud legacy of faithful service to humanity through academic excellence and fervent leadership. A humble product of Native and African American heritages, I came to value understanding why my life had purpose through what my family and community leaders instilled in me. Consequently, they fortified my early years with spiritual, physical, and mental conditioning to ensure I was vested with the proper tools to become a successful leader of men. A man is taught from birth about the responsibility one has to his brother. To be a brother infers a natural bond between two or more persons. As we grow older, the responsibility expands to include those outside of our biological group. Once we become men and are able to comprehend the aims and duties of manhood, we make decisions about brotherhood based on life experiences, traditions, and cultural values. This lays the foundation for fraternal brotherhood.

Fraternal brothers are those who accept the obligation to unconditionally love and support each other. Fraternal brotherhood is about committing to the needs of a brother throughout his life. It involves the care and support of his family. For some, this is defined as friendship. For others, the resolve is a fraternal relationship. As matured men, we have the moral and ethical responsibility to be there for one another as our physical and mental capacity permits. This too is indicative of brotherhood. Another component of being a brother is having the moral courage to hold a brother accountable for the things he does that does not measure up to the expected standards of the fraternal relationship. I say relationship because without a relationship between two or more men, there is no brotherhood. Men are not merely brothers because of DNA or fraternal membership. Brotherhood is an active qualification that requires periodic validation, strict examination, and routine certification.

The principles of brotherhood dictate that one must continually give without the condition of expecting anything in return. To be frank, the Alpha man gives with the fervency, zeal, and degree that he is guaranteed to experience the reciprocal. Alpha men are unconditionally committed to academic excellence. We work tirelessly to remove barriers to equity in education. For Alpha men, scholarship is more than a call to action; it is a lifelong commitment. As the local NAACP president, I helped to establish several memorial scholarships to ensure our youth had opportunities to rise above these barriers and equal the playing field.

These legacy scholarships honor African Americans who made notable contributions throughout the state of Hawaii and are named for Alice Augusta Ball (scientist), Dr. Alonzo DeMello (community leader and activist), Helene Eleanor Hale (politician), Dr. Donnis Hazel Thompson (educator), and William Henry Waddell, IV, VMD (educator and Buffalo Soldier). Additionally, I played an intentional role in teaching students, staffs, and administrations across the state about race and racism in education. I contribute by promoting excellence in education, including my own. I periodically lecture at local universities and schools, and regularly teach empowerment classes at the Oahu Women's Correctional Center and the Halawa Men's Prison. For several years, I tutored each week at Lehua Elementary School. I was honored to serve on the Hawaii State Department of Education Civil Rights Compliance Advisory Committee.

Likewise, I promote scholarships being awarded in each of the professional organizations in which I hold membership. I am a successful life skills coach, dedicated mentor, and effective business management consultant. In college I earned a Bachelor of Science in Business Management and a Master of Business Administration. Men of Alpha lead from the front. Our legacies are defined by our trailblazing efforts at the local, state, and national level. For nearly five decades, I have served as a leader in church, school, military, civil service, and civic groups. Some roles were more challenging than others. However, each opportunity became a catalyst to forge a legacy befitting the honor and integrity of those who paved the way for me to achieve.

For example, I am a life member on the NAACP and serve at several levels including national committees, National Board of Directors, state conference executive committee, and local branch president. In the performance of my duties, I resolved to take the principled stand based on the superlative examples of my predecessors like NAACP cofounder W.E.B. Dubois and NAACP chief legal counsel Thurgood Marshall. I routinely refer to the legacy of trailblazing men and mentors like Charles Hamilton Houston John Hope Franklin. Locally, I helped revitalize the Honolulu Hawaii

NAACP Branch and worked to expand our area of operations to include Guam, Japan, and Korea. We established the NAACP Lifetime Achievement Award for Distinguished Service, the Community Partnership Award, the Religious Leadership Award, and the Outstanding Youth Leadership Award. In recognition of the brave men and women who serve as exemplary military leaders, we established the Medgar Wiley Evers Outstanding Community Service Award, the Ida B. Wells-Barnett Meritorious Community Service Award, the Dr. Mary McLeod Bethune Inspirational Leadership Award, and the Thurgood Marshall Distinguished Leadership Award.

In Hawaii, I was one of the few African Americans to serve on the Board of Directors for the Japanese American Citizens League (JACL). The JACL is the counterpart to the NAACP with a primary objective of civil rights advocacy for Japanese Americans. I have been serving in that role for over a decade. I was appointed and honored to serve as a member of the U.S. Commission on Civil Rights State Advisory Committee. I served as the host the long-running NAACP Today show.

To expand and enrich professional organizations within our community, I helped organize and became a charter member of the first Blacks in Government Chapter in the state of Hawaii and Pacific Islands and served as its parliamentarian. I have been recognized for my efforts at all levels and from many agencies and organizations including the U.S. Equal Employment Opportunity Commission; U.S. Census Bureau; American Red Cross; Omega Psi Phi Fraternity, Incorporated; Hawaii Chapter of the Links, Incorporated; University of Hawaii; Chaminade University; and a host of government agencies.

The men of Alpha have never felt it a burden to extend their leadership talents beyond the House of Alpha. It has been my distinct honor to mentor good men made better who have earned the coveted title of double brother in Prince Hall Freemasonry and Shrinedom. In the Blue House, I served in every elected office in the lodge. As a Past Master, I have been elected to serve as Grand Junior Warden, Grand Lecturer, and Grand Comptroller in the Most Worshipful Prince Hall Grand Lodge of Hawaii. I played an integral role in growing the jurisdiction. I organized and chartered Doris Miller Lodge No. 6. I was elected to serve as Associate Patron in New Hope Lodge, Order of the Eastern Stars.

In the Scottish Rite side of Masonry, I helped to organize and charter Doris Miller Consistory No. 388 and served as charter Commander in Chief. I serve as the Grand Minister of State for the Council of Deliberation. In 2014, I was elevated to the 33rd degree, the last and final degree in Freemasonry Grand Inspector General. In the York Rite side of Masonry, I helped to organize and charter Mt. Moriah Council No. 4. In Shrinedom, I was elected to serve as Treasurer, Chief Rabin, and Illustrious Potentate and humbled as a Past Potentate to carry the title of Imperial Ambassador at Large.

Alpha men have been at the helm of defining moments in world history. We believe strongly in responsible citizenship and ethical public service. For me, leadership and public service came early in life. Long before I was able to vote, I was involved in the political arena and working on voter registration and voter education. My inspiration to achieve comes from the personal examples of the great scholars I read about as a child. In the ninth grade I served as editor of the school newspaper and in the tenth grade was elected and reelected to serve three one-year terms on City Council as a youth member.

My service was galvanized by the council's establishment of the "President's Award," and I became the council's first recipient. At the age of sixteen, I organized the local and district youth councils for my church and became the first president and began traveling across the country as a delegate to various conventions and conferences. The same year I was elected to a national office as Southeast Region Youth Council Treasurer. I served as a junior trustee in my local church at the age of seventeen.

Alpha men leave legacies of distinguished service as citizens of the state and proud defenders of democracy. I proudly spent over 26 years in the Navy serving on submarines and in the immediate office of the Secretary of the Navy. In the military, I continued to serve the community. Shortly after my naval career began, I was elected Vice President of the Protestant Gospel Service Congregation at the Fort Myer Chapel. While stationed in Northern California, I had the distinction of serving as one the youngest members on the Board of Trustees of the historic First African Methodist Episcopal Zion Church, San Francisco, California.

My civic engagement continued after arriving in Pearl Harbor, Hawaii, where I served as Vice President and President of the Navy and Marine Corps African American Heritage Association. I played an integral role in helping to expand our community and cultural engagement, particularity with the celebration of Black History Month and Juneteenth events. My service to humanity was acknowledged internationally when in 1998, I was appointed as one of two persons selected from the state of Hawaii to serve on the National Summit on Africa Commission and given the honor of working with former President Jimmy Carter. Alpha men recognize the need for African American mentors, and our legacy contains some of the most inspiring accounts of effective mentors. The legacy that was passed down to me has properly prepared me to be an effective mentor. The ability to go that extra mile and connect with society's future is one of the most rewarding experiences I have ever encountered.

You could say that it may even be addicting because of the natural high one gets from making a difference in someone's life. It is a feeling that cannot easily be explained in words. I became a mentor because I fully understood the value of being mentored. Pride in my culture and empowered by the legacy of my blackberry seed, I am committed to building a better society through mentorship. African American male mentors can have a great impact on the success or failure of today's youth. We have the ability to positively impact the quality, quantity, and protocols for youth development in our communities.

The example I was given demonstrated that mentoring was more than just checking a box for a meet-and-greet. The neighbors, teachers, preachers, and other faithful individuals who mentored me and other kids in my neighborhood took their roles very seriously. They were determined to achieve positive results. The measures of their success can easily be found in my several accomplishments. I could not have gotten the advanced college degrees, attained the esteemed positions, or mustered the wherewithal to stand before great audiences and speak with confidence had they not invested in my journey. I often draw a parallel between my youthful challenges and the challenges our young people face today. I engage them and while keeping it real; I work to bridge that great divide between the generations that diminished self-respect and respect for others. I make a concerted effort to help them find and hold on to the worth and value of the common good in all of God's creations.

Alpha mentors realize that it takes the entire village, and we owe it to future leaders of society to make sure they are properly prepared to lead and guide humanity. I am always mindful that a caring individual helped me set aside my pride so that I could be properly developed to lead future generations. As an Alpha man, I have the humble honor of carrying our legacy forward and effectively developing the next generation of mentors to do likewise. My blackberry seed legacy has taught me that no one is too young or too old to become a mentor or to be mentored. True mentorship is about giving of your time and talent not for personal gain but because you genuinely believe in the people you are mentoring. You care about them and you appreciate the opportunity for a healthy relationship that validates the Creator's intent that our legacy should illuminate a pathway for others to follow.

It has often been said that we are the product of our society. I am a great example of such an analogy. I grew up in Jervay projects. I came from a broken home. I faced social and economic challenges as a child. So why would I not be a good example of such an analogy? After all, this phrase is generally associated with ethnic minorities from the inner city. More often than not, it is associated as a negative stereotype. However, I have been known for defying the odds and proving the status quo wrong. ***I believe I am the product of my choices.*** My faith continues to affirm that where I have no control, God is in control; so, I do not have to accept that which is unacceptable. Only those who yield their will are defined by the statistics of devastation and failure. Consequently, I chose to work hard at rising above the stigmas and surrounding myself with positive influences.

The fact that I was trying to overcome these odds was noticed by the best and brightest in my community, and they saw to it that my struggle to achieve became part of their master plan. Accordingly, they opened an opportunity for me to achieve. I immediately enrolled in the college of mentorship and became a permanent student teacher. Every day is a day spent on its campus learning while I actively teach others to achieve and sustain. Alpha men are set apart from their contemporaries because they espouse the highest principles of leadership, mentorship, and citizenship. Their unquestionable faith allows them to confidently challenge the ills of society with courage and strength of character. Purposeful and value based, we stand as upright men forging legacies commensurate with the core tenants of our beloved fraternity.

Epilogue

"We Need to Leave a Legacy"

When I was a kid, I would see this group of individuals who stood out for all the right reasons. I soon learned that they were the more august men and women of the community. When I became an adult, I learned they were Prince Hall Masons and members of the Divine Nine or other professional organizations. As a child, I did not know about their personal affiliations with these groups, because they made their service to others their primary witness. They wore no special labels except a prominent light that emanated from within them representing the best the Creator had to offer future generations. What little wisdom I possessed, I was able to discern that it did not originate with them, nor were they willing to allow it to stop at their generation. This was my first introduction on how they proudly embraced their rich heritage, actively engaged and educated the community, and carefully passed on this proud blackberry seed legacy to future generations.

One of the greatest lessons my Grandma Ruth taught me is humility. I do not think that it originated with her; rather, somewhere along the way she decided it is a strong character trait we should pass on to future generations. I was raised to be effective in my daily encounters with others. Given that I never expected to be famous or have a lot of followers, I was always amazed as to why these good men and women stepped up and took care of kids like me. They worked hard and represented the best in our community. They were the ones who stood by me on difficult days and applauded me in rewarding times. I owe these men and women a great debt of gratitude because they really made a difference in my life. Because of their faithful dedication and substantial investment in my well-being, I am committed to giving back to future generations all that they gave and then some.

Three of my father's sons are Greek Fraternity Brothers. I have the distinction of carrying the Alpha Phi Alpha Fraternity, Incorporated torch. For me there was no other choice, and all that I do in life validates I made the right choice. At times I pondered if I would ever achieve the level of influence they commanded with such calm demeanor. I quietly noticed my family's absence in these prestigious affiliations. Clearly, it was not because they were opposed to them; we had just not engaged their membership. Thus, I was encouraged to take advantage of the opportunity and keep the pathway open for others. After all, the opportunity to carry forth their great legacies was now open to any and all. I am grateful that the research on my family revealed men and women of humble beginnings with lives rich in service to others and a strong faith in God. These men and women took pride in toiling in the fields to provide for their families and communities. Their basic lessons have guided me in my daily service to others. These lessons teach us that a legacy is not always about becoming famous or having great wealth. Instead, the moral of their stories teaches us that we must leave a legacy that shows we did our best, and in doing so we have shown gratitude for our past, present, and future.

As the chief steward of this blessed creation, I am compelled to respond to the elders whispers. I hear them saying, ***"What did you do to help move our legacy forward? What bridges of life did you help our people crossover? Did you make sure future blackberry seeds will take pride in our heritage?"*** Once I learned of my proud legacy, I immediately began the process of developing protocols—properly put in place protocols—for future generations to address the ancestors' call. Our history is far too important not to pass on. We must take the time to share the lessons we learned. Otherwise, they will never know the great sacrifices and toilsome journeys our people went through so that we could be at our present place and enjoy what we have today.

The knowledge imparted along the way will empower them to overcome disparate treatments; brave indignities, racism, and oppression; and boldly forge a pathway toward peaceful attainment of justice and equality for all. I am grateful that our family taught us the value of respecting our past to bring it forward. Likewise, I believe that every person contributes to our society, and their contributions warrant appropriate recognition. Fortitude and tenacity are leadership traits the elders passed down to my generation. I reflect on the tough times they endured. In every community, there are a few leaders who stand out and rise to the occasion. They stand out because they take charge of situations and conditions and expect nothing in return except the humble acknowledgment that they did their best.

Their example gave me the desire to push through the tough times and achieve. I recall someone asking if I thought I had achieved greatness. I thought about Grandma Ruth, the elders, and the inspiring men and women at church, school, and the community growing up. I humbly replied that I do not think I ever thought about being great, just effective. I mentioned that I have felt this way since I was a small boy in elementary school reading stories about famous African Americans.

I was also asked about being a legend and trailblazer. I do not consider myself a legend or trailblazer. However, I have worked tirelessly to promote justice and equality for all persons, perpetuate the legacy of African Americans and other minorities across the United States, and help to validate the belief that together we can make a difference in our community. Likewise, I am committed to putting the neighbor back into the neighborhood. I do not think that qualifies me to be a legend, as I expect all citizens of this great Democracy to do the same. I am simply committed to ensuring that their right to *be all they can be* is protected.

Some may say that I am prominent because of the positions I held or hold in politics, civil rights, or fraternal organizations. I serve and continue to serve at the will and pleasure of the people who appoint, elect, and reelect me to these positions. It is indeed an honor to serve in positions of leadership and earn the title of "social justice advocate." I just feel like it is my duty, given the tremendous burdens our elders bore without complaint. I am considered a good leader because the organizations I led achieved successes, effectively served our community, and took care of constituents.

Sometimes, I encounter difficult days. Then I reflect on Grandma Ruth; I pause and gently take it in. She made me proud to belong to this great body of humankind, especially African and Native Americans. She is the reason I am so committed to making future generations proud of the service I render. We do a disservice to future generations when we fail to teach them about their origins and the contributions of their ancestors. For thousands of years, our African and Native American ancestors told their children of their father's father and the legacy of their rich heritage.

These stories instilled hope for future generations and fortified cultural pride. I cannot be content with just passing on to my children and grandchildren that one day our ancestors crossed the great Atlantic on a slave ship or were driven across the plains in a trail of blood. I need to share how they suffered through the tragedies of slavery and hundreds of years of oppression and here is where we are today. I need to ensure they know how to cross the bridges of life to a place called cultural pride. Yes, I must instill in them an understanding of the *before*—the years we spent as great Kings, Queens, and Tribal Chiefs.

Regardless of our ethnic background, we should continue to share these stories. As parents, we need to research our family heritage and teach future generations so that they have something to pass on beside what social media teaches as an "actual" depiction of our history and cultural heritage. By the way, let us not forget the role of faith in building and sustaining our legacy. Faith is an incredible instrument when combined with fortitude. Together they define our character and propel our legacy. It is this fiber that kicks in when all else gives way and we are not cognizant of the why or where. When the four seasons of our life concludes, it's about the legacy we leave.

I have several heroes who inspired me to achieve, and I believe learning about their legacies will help forge new and inspiring legacies. It is easier to live a legacy when you can relate to the heroes who paved the way for you to leave a legacy. During an interview on my NAACP Today Show, a young man stated his hero was Michael Jordan. Before I had the opportunity to inquire as to why he considered him a hero, he boldly proclaimed support for the positive aspects of Michael Jordan's life that inspired him, and suggested others be encouraged to achieve by doing the same.

This mindset is critical to forging a legacy because once you are able to extract the positive character traits of an individual and emulate them in your life, you better fortify your foundation. Others will see this model and want to follow you on a path to success. This is especially important in minority communities. Legacy building does not belong to any one race, class, or culture of people. Our legacies must be celebrated because there is no facet of the modern habitat that we have not played a significant role in shaping. My job is to forge new legacies that give honor to the past and hope for the future. This is the universal blackberry seed legacy, and one we are committed to preserving.

About the Author

Alphonso Braggs, MBA

Mr. Braggs was born and raised in Wilmington, North Carolina and served three consecutive terms on the Wilmington City Council as a Youth Member. After graduating from John T. Hoggard high school, he joined the U.S. Navy and completed more than 26 years of honorable service before retiring in January 2004. He served onboard nuclear submarines sailing throughout the Atlantic, Pacific, Indian, and Arctic Oceans, completing 10 arduous deployments. After retiring, he served as Operations Director for Angel Network Charities, Inc. before returning to federal government service at the Treasury and Defense Departments. A devout social justice advocate, he is committed to defending civil and human rights. He is a life member and current president of the Honolulu-Hawaii NAACP Branch overseeing operations in Japan, Korea, Guam, and Hawaii and serves on the Board of Directors, Japanese American Citizens League Honolulu Chapter. He is the former host of the "NAACP Today" television show. He serves on the National NAACP Board of Directors and the U.S. Commission on Civil Rights State Advisory Committee. Mr. Braggs holds membership in several professional and fraternal organizations including Alpha Phi Alpha Fraternity, Inc. and is honored to serve in senior leadership positions in Prince Hall Freemasonry and Shrinedom. Mr. Braggs holds a Bachelor of Science in Business Management and a Master of Business Administration. Fully engaged in community building, he mentors youth and aspiring entrepreneurs. He is a devoted life skills coach and facilitator for the Women's and Men's Prisons. He is a proud father and grandfather and loves the great outdoors and writing.

Alphonso Braggs founded the Blackberry Seed Legacy Foundation (BSLF) to perpetuate the blackberry seed legacy and to help develop future leaders through seminars, educational activities, events, and cultural programs. The BSLF is a nonprofit that awards academic scholarships and provides counseling and mentoring services to aspiring entrepreneurs in business planning, management, and professional development. A portion of the proceeds from this book will be donated to the BSLF.

References and Sources

1. Ancestral research conducted at the Batts Cemetery, Browntown, North Carolina. Confirmed the location of family members' burial places, collected photos, and dates; June 2004.
2. Ancestral research conducted at the Church of Jesus Christ of Latter Day Saints Research Library in Salt Lake City, UT. Their archives contain one of the largest collections of African American records. Confirmed family records on births, names, deaths, and relationships.
3. Ancestral research conducted at U.S. Library of Congress Archives, Washington, D.C. Confirmed family records on births, names, deaths, and relationships; July 2006.
4. Excerpted remarks from lecture(s) given at the Chaminade University, Hawaii Campus, Honolulu, English Literature Classes
5. Excerpted remarks from lectures given at the Hawaii State Department of Public Safety, Women's Community Correctional Center, Kailua, Hawaii, NAM Empowerment Classes
6. Excerpted remarks from speech(es) given at the African Americans on Maui Association, Maui, Hawaii, Cultural Celebration
7. Excerpted remarks from speech(es) given at the Brigham Young University, Laie, Hawaii, Cultural Celebration
8. Excerpted remarks from speech(es) given at the Center of Deliverance Church of God In Christ, Wahiawa, Hawaii, Cultural Celebration
9. Excerpted remarks from speech(es) given at the Department of Defense, U.S. Navy, Commander, U.S, Pacific Fleet, Pearl Harbor, Hawaii, Cultural Celebration
10. Excerpted remarks from speech(es) given at the Department of Defense, U.S. Pacific Command, Honolulu, Hawaii, Cultural Celebration
11. Excerpted remarks from speech(es) given at the Department of Defense, U.S. Navy, Commander, Navy Region Hawaii, Pearl Harbor, Hawaii, Cultural Celebration
12. Excerpted remarks from speech(es) given at the Department of Defense, U.S. Navy, Commander, Joint Base Pearl Harbor-Hickam, Pearl Harbor, Hawaii, Cultural Celebration
13. Excerpted remarks from speech(es) given at the Department of Defense, U.S. Navy, USS Port Royal, Pearl Harbor, Hawaii, Cultural Celebration
14. Excerpted remarks from speech(es) given at the Department of Defense, U.S. Navy, USS Chaffee, Pearl Harbor, Hawaii, Cultural Celebration
15. Excerpted remarks from speech(es) given at the Department of Defense, U.S. Navy, Afloat Training Group, Middle Pacific, Pearl Harbor, Hawaii, Cultural Celebration
16. Excerpted remarks from speech(es) given at the Department of Defense, U.S. Navy, Naval Computer and Telecommunications Area Master Station Pacific, Wahiawa, Hawaii, Cultural Celebration
17. Excerpted remarks from speech(es) given at the Department of Defense, U.S. Navy, Naval Operational Support Center, Pearl Harbor, Hawaii, Cultural Celebration
18. Excerpted remarks from speech(es) given at the Department of Defense, U.S. Army, Commander, U.S, Army Pacific, Fort Shafter, Hawaii, Cultural Celebration
19. Excerpted remarks from speech(es) given at the Department of Defense, U.S. Army, Tripler Army Medical Center, Honolulu, Hawaii, Cultural Celebration
20. Excerpted remarks from speech(es) given at the Department of Defense, U.S. Army, Schofield Barracks, Wahiawa, Hawaii, Cultural Celebration
21. Excerpted remarks from speech(es) given at the Department of Defense, U.S. Army, Schofield Barracks Army Medical Clinic, Wahiawa, Hawaii, Cultural Celebration
22. Excerpted remarks from speech(es) given at the Department of Defense, Defense Logistics Center Pacific, Pearl Harbor, Hawaii, Cultural Celebration

23. Excerpted remarks from speech(es) given at the Department of Homeland Security, Naturalization and Immigration Office, Honolulu Hawaii, Cultural Celebration
24. Excerpted remarks from speech(es) given at the Department of Justice, U.S. Federal Bureau of Prisons Hawaii, Honolulu, Hawaii, Cultural Celebration
25. Excerpted remarks from speech(es) given at the Hawaii Chapter of the Links, Inc. Honolulu, Hawaii, Cultural Celebration
26. Excerpted remarks from speech(es) given at the Hawaii Department of Education, Moanalua High School, Honolulu, Hawaii, Cultural Celebration
27. Excerpted remarks from speech(es) given at the Hawaii Department of Education, Radford High School, Honolulu, Hawaii, Cultural Celebration
28. Excerpted remarks from speech(es) given at the Hawaii Department of Education, Waipahu High School, Waipahu, Hawaii, Social Studies Project
29. Excerpted remarks from speech(es) given at the Hawaii Jurisdiction Convocation Service, Church of God In Christ, Wahiawa, Hawaii, Cultural Celebration
30. Excerpted remarks from speech(es) given at the Punahou School, Honolulu, Hawaii, Cultural Celebration
31. Family Bible Record belonging to Rosa Bell Nixon Hansley with records of maternal family members dates of birth and death.
32. General Douglas McArthur farewell speech ending 52 years of military service on April 19, 1951 to a Joint Session of Congress. The transcript of his speech is on file in several places. I consulted the one on file at the Truman Library.
33. http://docsouth.unc.edu/church/moorej/moore.html
34. http://firstAfrican Methodist Episcopal Zionionchurchsanfrancisco160.blogspot.com/p/history.html
35. http://www.African Methodist Episcopal Zion.org/
36. http://www.buffalosoldier.net/CIVILWARAFRICAN-AMERICANMEDALOFHONORRECIPIENTS.htm
37. http://www.civilwar.org/education/history/faq/;
38. http://www.history.army.mil/moh/index.html;
39. http://www.loc.gov/teachers/classroommaterials/presentationsandactivities/presentations/timeline/civilwar/aasoldrs/;
40. http://www.pbs.org/wgbh/americanexperience/features/general-article/death-numbers/;
41. http://www.varickmemorial.org/contentpages.aspx?parentnavigationid=24647&navigationId=24652&viewcontentpageguid=c2217510-2892-4551-95b1-f74671c7efe2
42. Journal of the Old New Hanover Genealogical Society, Volume 1 5, Number 1, Winter 2003. Provided verification and clarification of the issues with changes in geographical boundary changes for lines, townships, county annexes, and other concerns my ancestral residences reported in census records.
43. Multiple 2014 telephonic and Social Media Interviews with Ms. Vanessa Green. Her Great-Great-Grandmother Mary Bragg and my Great-Grandfather William Henry Bragg, Sr. were sister and brother. She shared verifiable research done on the family history and provided connections and documents to further my research and documentation of our family legacy.
44. Navy History – USS George C. Marshall (SSBN654)
45. North Carolina State Department of Health, Bureau of Vital Statistics, Certificates of Death. Obtained numerous verifications of birth, residence, age, and family cultural.
46. North Carolina, Birth Indexes, 1800-2000
47. Oakland Tribune Article, October 29, 1972, Highlights of the 1940's performers. http://web.archive.org/web/20120209175145/http://www.sfradiomuseum.com/audio/ksfo/1972/Trib_Pop-Chronicles-Article-2_1972.pdf
48. Oral and telephonic interviews with Idell Nixon Braggs. She is my mother. She attested to dates of birth, death, residences, and family unit structures, and environments.
49. Oral and telephonic interviews with Professor Earl Braggs, 2014 - 2015.
50. Oral and telephonic interviews with Sylvia Nixon Hyman, 1998 - 2015.
51. Oral and video interviews with Mary D. Morrison. June 2004. Her brother Porter Nixon is my mother's father. She provided confirmation of family members, places of birth, dates, and cultural environment, and other family information. She was 80 at the time of the interview.
52. Oral and video interviews with Mrs. Margaret Simmons. June 2004. Her father Dave Nixon and my maternal Great Grandfather Louis Nixon were brothers. She provided confirmation of their biological relationship, place of birth, and other family information. She was 84 at the time of the interview.
53. Oral interview with Mrs. Emily Bradley. August 2015. Her brother Edward Earl Bragg is my father. Her father is William Henry Bragg, Jr. She attested to ancestral information on the Bragg family.
54. Oral interview with Mrs. Emily Bradley. June 2004. Her brother Edward Earl Bragg is my father. Her father is William Henry Bragg, Jr. She provided photos and information on family.

55. Oral interview with Mrs. Evalene Bragg. June 2004. Her husband Alfred Bragg, Sr. Grandfather Charley Bragg and my Great-Grandfather William Henry Bragg, Sr. are brothers. Her sister Ruth E. Spicer Bragg is my maternal grandmother. She provided substantial information on the family and the cultural for both sides of my father's family. She was 94 at the time of the interview.
56. Oral interviews with Dr. John Hope Franklin. He was a guest speaker at several forums in Hawaii. He spoke at the University of Hawaii and Chaminade University. I was able to speak with him on these occasions and gain valuable wisdom and insight on his perspectives surrounding the African American culture. I was honored to have lunch with him and "breakfast time" on a return visit. John Hope Franklin was a highly esteemed historian and author, known for his scholarship that focused on Southern history and racial politics.
57. Oral interviews with Mary D. Morrison. August 2015. Her brother Porter Nixon is my mother's father. She provided confirmation of family members, places of birth, dates, and cultural environment, and other family information.
58. Oral interviews with Mary D. Morrison. December 2018. Her brother Porter Nixon is my mother's father. Discussions held following the passing of my mother. She provided confirmation of family members, places of birth, dates, and cultural environment, and other family information.
59. Oral interviews with Posey W. Johnson, 2004 - 2019. She was my Sunday School teach and mentor. She provided substantive confirmation of the AME Zion church and the formation and my youth engagement.
60. Oral, telephonic, and television interviews with Dr. James Oliver Horton. He was a guest on my television show the NAACP Today Show in Honolulu Hawaii. He was the keynote speaker for our local NAACP Dr. Martin Luther King, Jr. Ball. Dr. Horton is the Benjamin Banneker Professor of American Studies and History at George Washington University and Historian Emeritus of the Smithsonian Institution's National Museum of American History
61. Research on African Americans and the Civil War. Reviewed the Library of Congress, Public Broadcasting Station, Civil War History Sites, U.S. Army History, U.S. Navy History, Buffalo Soldier Association, and other sources.
62. Telephonic Interviews with Mr. Thomas Green. September 2014. His Great-Grandmother Mary Bragg and my Great Grandfather William Henry Bragg, Sr. were sister and brother. He provided first account of blood relatives and the connection of downlink siblings. He gave information relating to cultural environment and family structure.
63. The Fannie Lou Hamer, Rosa Parks, And Coretta Scott King Voting Rights Act Reauthorization And Amendments Act Of 2006 signed into law by President George W. Bush. http://georgewbush-whitehouse.archives.gov/news/releases/2006/07/20060727-1.html
64. U.S. Census Report, 1880. Obtained verification of birth, residence, age, and family cultural.
65. U.S. Census Report, 1890. Obtained verification of birth, residence, age, and family cultural.
66. U.S. Census Report, 1900. Obtained verification of birth, residence, age, and family cultural.
67. U.S. Census Report, 1910. Obtained verification of birth, residence, age, and family cultural.
68. U.S. Census Report, 1920. Obtained verification of birth, residence, age, and family cultural.
69. U.S. Census Report, 1930. Obtained verification of birth, residence, age, and family cultural.
70. U.S. Census Report, 1940. Obtained verification of birth, residence, age, and family cultural.
71. U.S. Census Report, 1940. Obtained verification of birth, residence, age, and family cultural.
72. U.S. Draft Registration Cards filed in the State of North Carolina. Obtained verification of birth, residence, age, and family cultural.
73. U.S. World War II Army Enlistment Records, 1938-1946
74. U.S., Find A Grave Index, 1600s-Current
75. United States Supreme Court Opinion on 1965 Voting Rights Act in the SHELBY COUNTY, ALABAMA *v.* HOLDER, ATTORNEY GENERAL, ET AL. http://www.supremecourt.gov/opinions/12pdf/12-96_6k47.pdf
76. Video interview with Mrs. Rosa Sidberry. June 2004. She was the neighbor to my Great Grandmother Hattie Brown Nixon. She was 106 at the time of the interview.

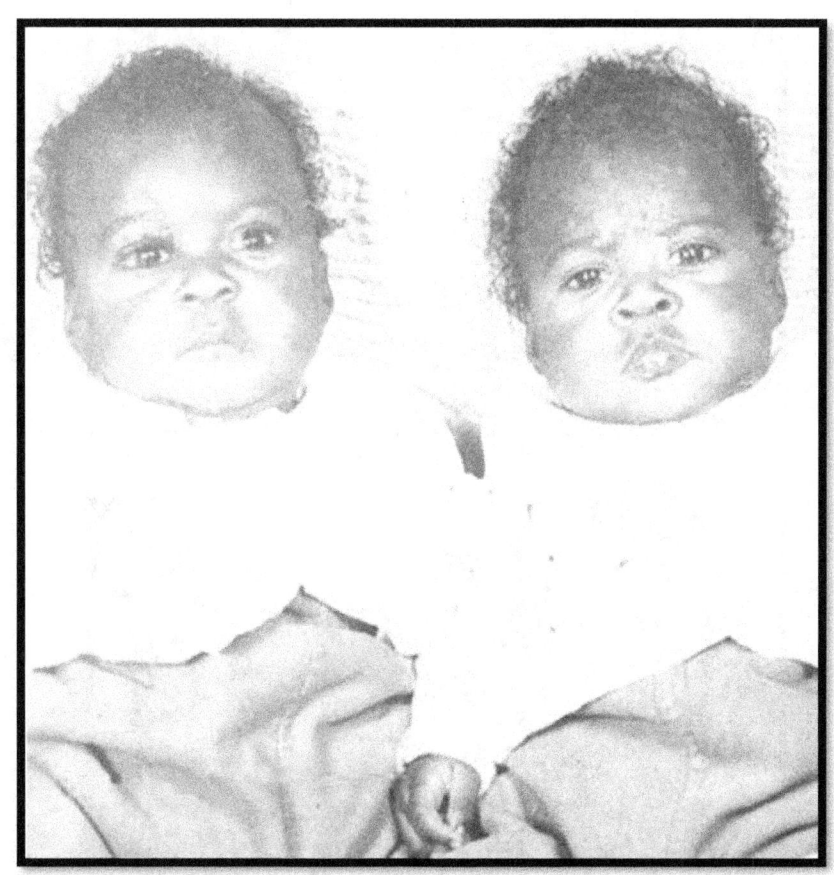

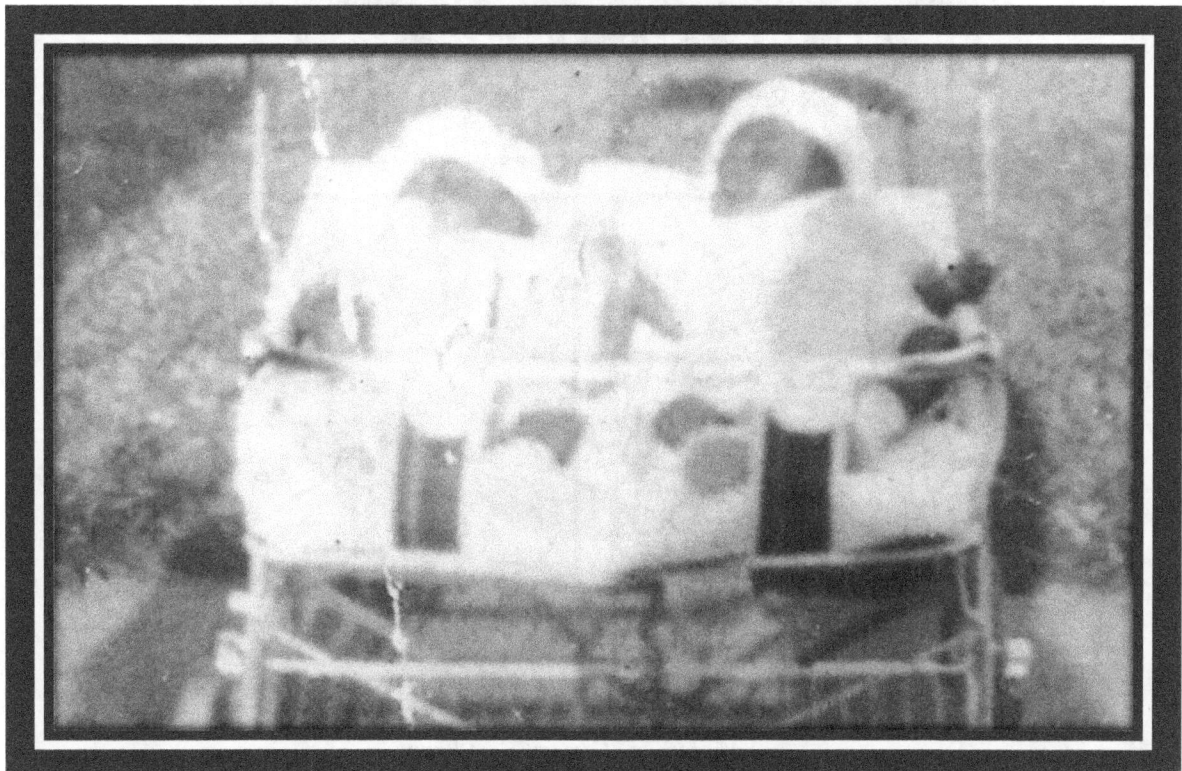

Alonzo and Alphonso Braggs, 1960

(top) My father, Edward Earl Bragg
(bottom) my paternal grandmother and paternal grandfather, Ruth E. Spicer Bragg, William Henry Bragg, Jr.

(top) This is a priceless treasure I found on my paternal great-grandfather, William Henry Bragg Sr. It revealed invaluable information about my blackberry seed legacy. (bottom) my paternal grandfather's William Henry Bragg Jr. selective service registration card.

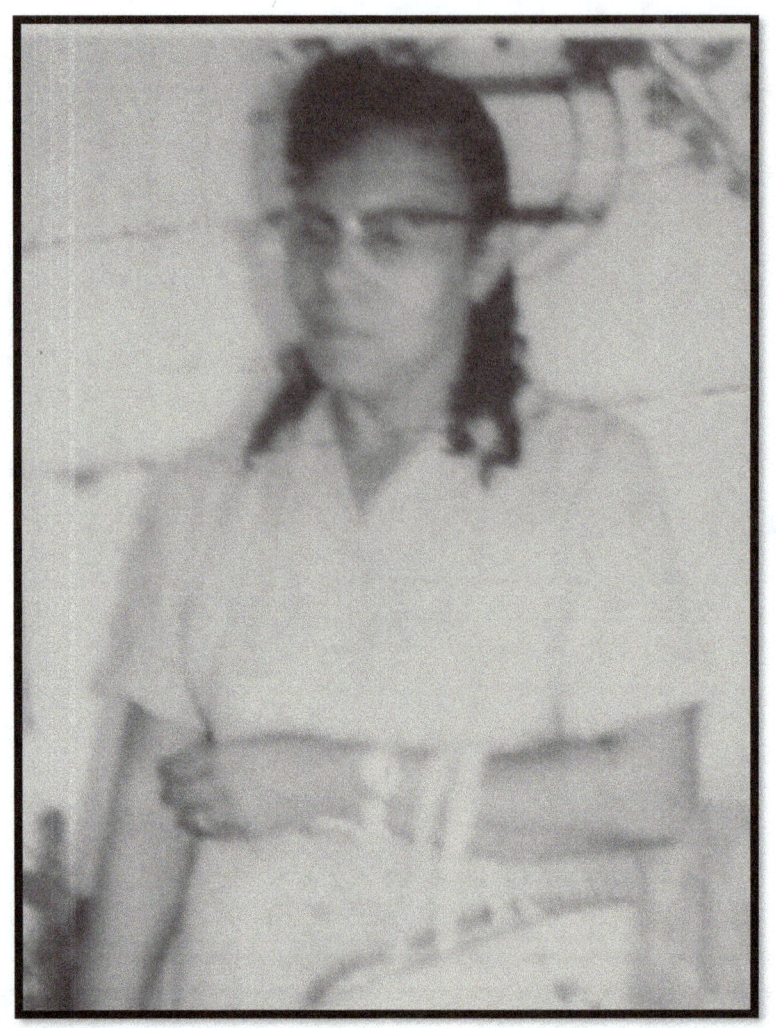

(top) my paternal great-aunt, Bessie Bragg.
(bottom) my maternal grandmother, Rosabell Nixon Hansley.

(above) Family photo of my mom Idell, sister Monica, brothers Lee and Alonzo.
(bottom) One of the most memorable moments I captured on film of Grandma Ruth was in the late summer of 1978. She had been very sick and it seemed like she got special energy for this day. My mother prepared a special meal and my sister Monica and brother Lee came along. Joining us for the fellowship was her roommate at the nursing home. This would be the last time I would get to talk to her. God called her home a few weeks later.
Sleep on loving grandma, your labors were not in vain!

(top) My mother Idell Braggs and sister Monica Braggs, (below) My maternal great-grandmother Hattie Brown Nixon and maternal great-great grandmother Caroline Brown

(top left and middle) brothers Tyrone Romell Braggs and Earl Sherman Braggs. (top right) Alfred Bragg, Jr., my first cousin who served in Vietnam. He was very talented and played in Bo Diddley's band while living in New York. He died far too young and was very close to my brother Earl. (middle left) visiting with my paternal Aunt Emily Bradley, (my father's only sister). (middle right) Evalena Spicer Bragg (Grandma Ruth's baby sister) (She married my cousin Alfred Bragg, son of Uncle Charley Bragg). She lived to see 102. This was from a visit in 2004. (bottom) In 2004, I got to visit Mrs. Rosa Sidbury while vacationing in North Carolina. She was a spirited 106 at the time.

(top) The historic "Browntown School" where so many of my elders and ancestors went to school. It is located on Highway 17 in Browntown, Hampstead, North Carolina, just across the street from Mama Hattie's home.
(bottom) Pages from our family bible.

My Blackberry Seed Legacy –
Unfinished Conversations with My Father

(top) St John Disciples of Christ Church was my first church home. The church and its teachings were introduced to me by Grandma Ruth. This was the Bragg's family church. I spent many a Sunday here as a kid and I said goodbye to Grandma Ruth at this church. Some of my best times at St John included the Sunday night singing and fellowship. (bottom) The maternal side of my family attended Christian Chapel Baptist Church. It was located just around the corner from St John, my church. This was Mama Hattie's church. As children growing up in Hampstead we visited here often. The last time I visited was for her homegoing service. It was here that she would share her favorite song, "This Little Light of Mine."

(top left) I took my son Andre home to visit with relatives. I wanted him to know the legacy of his blackberry seed. Here he is meeting Cousin Margaret. Her dad and my maternal grandmother, Rosa Bell Nixon Hansley, dad were brothers. She shared stories of our ancestors and our proud heritage. We were just regular kin folk visiting. She said baby, yall special kin. She got dressed like she was heading to church with her pearls on for our visit. She told Andre, "Son, I'm so proud of your daddy." She then squeezed my hand and gazed. Her silence was both piercing and rewarding. She was the Chair of Stewardess Board No 1 at church. She told mama that she would be our church class leader when we joined. A job she performed faithfully long after I moved away from home.

(top right) Our beloved Bishop Herbert Bell Shaw, Sr., the presiding prelate of the AME Zion church and his sweet wife Mrs. M. Ardell Shaw. They were exceptional mentors. He was one of the most approachable global leaders I knew. He had a commanding presence. He was also the grandmaster of masons for North Carolina.

(boottom left) My second church home was St Andrew AME Zion Church located on the corner of 9th and Marstellar Streets, Wilmington, North Carolina. It was just a two-block walk from our home in Jervay and one block away from Cousin Margaret Simmons' house. I have fond memories of her walking down the street on her way to church in her Sunday best.

(bottom right) The Fellowship Hall is located just behind the main sanctuary. It was the original church and served many purposes including social events and vacation bible school. I recall the driveway between the church and the hall where the bishop would park his gold colored Cadillac. The hall was later named the Rev. Robert W. Johnson Fellowship Hall

(top) A photo taken in the mid 1970s, is a superb representation of Zion's fervent and faithful. These ladies sat in the "Amen Corner" and prepared the altar and Holy sacriment on first Sundays and other special services. One would be hard pressed to replace such a starward group of church mothers. They now rest from their labors. (pictured l-r are Mrs. Flossie Harris, Mrs. Amelia Moore, Mrs. Margaret Simmons, Mrs. Dorothy Gibbs, and Mrs. Carrie Mae Nixon and Rev. Johnson) (inset) The Junior Choir of St Andrew. (l-r) Mrs. Posey Johnson, me, Lavanda Nixon, Romana Nixon, Rev. Robert W. Johnson, James Nixon, Brenda McCoy, Vincent McCoy, and Margarite McKnight). Mrs. Posey W. Johnson was our choir director. Mrs. Audrey Session was our organist. I loved singing in the church. My first church solo was performed at St. Andrew. I sang, "If I Can Help Somebody." The Junior Choir sung on second Sunday mornings.

(bottom left) Rev. Robert W. Johnson was the pastor and Mrs. Posey W. Johnson was the first lady. Rev. and Mrs. Johnson provided great support during my upbringing.

(bottom right) Visiting with Mrs. Johnson while home on vacation. Mrs. Johnson taught 6th grade at William Hooper Elementary right across the hall from my class and kept a close eye on me. In all of these years, her nuturing has never faded. Humbled by her selfless love and mentorship, I am equally committed to honoring her life and legacy.

(top left) One of my most beloved joys at the Fort Myer Gospel Service was ushering. My brother Fred Clark and I standing outside at the front doors of the historic Fort Myer Chapel on Sunday usher duty. We had fun trying to come up with matching outfits. We remembered the ushers would be matching in church back home. (top right) Our summers at Fort Myer were filled with fun trips to nearby theme parks and other activities. (l-r: Sandra, Cathy, Viola, Faye, Fred, and Ken) (middle) Members of Holy Light United Baptist Church gather for a photo after a wedding. (l-r) Celeste, Cathy, Rev. Vaughan, Larry, and Teal) (bottom left) Ministers Bruce and Vera James, another one of my oldest and dearest friends. He was my protector and became my lifelong friend! (bottom right) Celebrating her birthday with friends. I was blessed to be the godfather for their first child.

(top) It was also at Fort Myer that I met my beloved Marsha Walker
(below) One of my longest and dearest friends for life is Rev. Victor Patrick Blair.

(top left) After leaving the Washington, DC area, it was important to find a church to worship. As expected the folks back home let us know we had a church in a nearby town. We soon began fellowshipping at Walls Temple AME Zion Church, New London, Connecticut. I quickly accepted the fact that we had found a new church home. It felt so good to be back in Zion. (top right) In 1989, I got notice that it was time to transfer again to a new location. This happened just as I was getting comfortable with my new church family. I made the journey cross country to the West Coast and once again I transferred my church membership. This time to the historic First AME Zion Church, San Francisco, California. (middle) One of the highest honors bestowed upon me while serving at First Church was the opportunity to sing in concert on behalf of the Stewardess Board. Here I am with our pastor Rev. John E. Watts (far right) along with the backup singers. (bottom left) In 1992, I was given the opportunity to transfer to beautiful Hawaii. I would spend most of my time in fellowship at Trinity Missionary Baptist Church. My son Andre visited the island and joined me for one of their worship services. (bottom right) Although it was a new location, I was still expected to serve the community. I have had the honor of speaking across the state at multiple platforms such as the Black History Month speaker at the Honolulu Seven Day Adventist Church. I was grateful to share the program with Rev. Dr. Dwight E. Cook (Trinity Missionary Baptist Church) and the famed singer and musician David Swanson.

Another special blessing from God is my baby girl Allyson Ruth Braggs (the guardian). She is named for Grandma Ruth. She honored me with that proud parent moment graduating high school with honors. She maintained that distinction throughout college while earning four degrees. Words have yet to be written to express this father's pride.

I always enjoy my visits with the kids and grands. They were never long enough so we always captured the precious memories. I was excited that Andre Braggs (the conservator) has blessed me with three grandkids, and they are growing fast. A father cannot ask for more than a good mother for the grandkids and a hard working son of three beautiful children. I am beyond blessed and immensely proud.

Another one of God's unmerited blessings, Francklyn Celestin (the professor). Wise beyond his age, he is a scholar of life's greatest lessons. I am blessed to learn from my blackberry seeds. I treasure these opportunities with the utmost respect and love.

So proud of my mini-me Ryan Ibrahim (the architect). He has never missed an opportunity to remind me of my God given purpose. He constantly challenges me to aspire and inspire. I am definitely a better man because of his commitment to see the Creator's designs perfected.

As enlightened men, we are to illuminate a path for future legacies. I am grateful for the privilege to help prepare future leaders like Khyri Baker through mentoring and teaching life skills. So proud of his many accomplishments.

(top left) African Americans represent about 3 percent of the population in Hawaii. We are all family. Spending quality time with two of my dear sisters from another mother, Carolyn Floyd-Johnson, and Jewel McDonald. (top right) Celebrating our future with NAACP Vice President Kim Alston and Representative Cedric Gates at our annual Youth in the Park event. (middle left) To serve this present age is truly my calling to fulfill. Among the many honors I have had bestowed upon me is serving as president for the Honolulu Hawaii NAACP. Celebrating with officers Carlo Davis, Jolene Lau, Jewel McDonald, Anita Motte, Yolanda Johnson, Mel Colquitt, and Richard Robinson. (middle right) I served as a television host for several years including the "NAACP Today Show." One of the shows featured the senior leadership of the U.S. Census Bureau and we discussed the importance of participating in the 2010 U.S. Census. (bottom left) One of my greatest inspirations is also my Alpha Phi Alpha Fraternity Brother Dr. John Hope Franklin. It was one thing to know about the man and to study his amazing accomplishments. However, I felt especially blessed to have had exclusive audiences, including the opportunity to interview him. (bottom right) In the presence of greatness with Barack Obama. Like many men of color, I hoped our paths would cross. This was the first of several. I have been blessed to meet and greet several U.S. Presidents: Reagan, the elder Bush, and Clinton. I served on a commission with Carter. However, this one was a cut above the rest. He has a calming presence. He was gracious and acted like we had known each other for years.

(top) These are many wonderful memories I have serving as an NAACP leader. They are among the most treasured. Honored to host the famed Tuskegee Airman at the annual Honolulu Black Nurses Gala. (middle left) Presenting the first NAACP Lifetime Achievement Award for Distinguished Service to Representative Helene Hale along with Judge Sandra Simms and Attorney Daphne Barbee-Wooten. (bottom) attending NAACP national convention with branch members.

(below) One of several African American Complete Count Committee events of the 2010 Census with Regina Williams, John Boyd, Dewitt Greenwood, and his grandson. (above) Whenever a gentleman is in the presence of a lady, he cannot help but smile. This esteemed WWII veteran was our first honoree at the Military Leadership Awards Luncheon. Thank you for your service. (below) One of the many active duty honorees at our annual Outstanding Military Leadership Awards Luncheon.

(top) Hosting the NAACP's Annual Rev. Dr. Martin Luther King, Jr. Awards Gala. Among our most distinguished guests attending were (l-r) Past Imperial Potentate Donald Parks, Deputy Imperial Potentate Rick Julian, Hawaii Grandmaster of Masons Howard Covington, and Past Imperial Potentate Homer Buchannan. (middle) When given the opportunity to lead an organization, we should leave it better than when we started. Here we are following an initiation ceremony for 15 nobles. (bottom left) Illustrious Potentate donating to the local American Diabetes Association Honolulu Chapter on behalf of Takbir Temple. Deeply humbled by the impact our temple made on the institution and this community. (bottom right) While serving as the Potentate, I rode ole "Clyde" at one of our annual Labor Day Boat Rides in Honolulu. This one was a memorable event with over 500 guests underway.

(top) While serving as the Right Worshipful Grand Junior Warden I organized the annual Prince Hall Day Celebration onboard the historic Battleship Missouri Memorial. The Honorable Will Espero, Hawaii State Senate was the guest speaker. (middle left) This was a very proud day for Brothers Ray Williams, Richard Jeanpierre, Mario Tarver, and Nicholas Graham as they were raised to the sublime degree of a Master Mason. These are just a few men who became "Good Men Made Better." I had the tremendous honor of mentoring their class from start to finish. Each has climbed the ladder of success in their respective fields. I am very pleased to see that the return on investment is paying high dividends. (middle right) Throughout my term as Worshipful Master, I can honestly say that I traveled very few places without my faithful officers at my side and always there was Treasurer Willie Clark and my right hand and faithful aide, Senior Deacon Ronnie Barnes. We believed in community service and here we are in the kitchen where we fed the homeless at the River of Life Mission in Chinatown, Honolulu, Hawaii. This was a collaborative service project put together by our sister chapter, New Hope Chater No. 2 under the leadership of Worthy Matron Bridget Terry. (below left) (l-r) Junior Warden William Watts, Chaplain Richard Robinson, Grandmaster Linwood Richardson, and three school officials. Our lodge started a partnership with the elementary school to donate backpacks loaded with school supplies. New Hope Lodge No. 3 donated over 100 backpacks. (bottom right) I have been blessed to serve as a mentor in and out of the lodge. (l-r) Kimathi Clark, Jerry Brooks, Salvador Torres, and Damall Martin.

Charter Commander In Chief for Doris Miller Consistory No. 388 Valley of Pearl City, Orient of Hawaii

Scottish Rite – PHA, Grand Inspector General Alphonso Braggs, 33º

Aloha Chapter, Mt Moriah Council, & Hugues de Payens Commandery York Rite (Hawaii Jurisdiction, PHA)

(top) My installation ceremony for Worshipful Master, Class of 2011 Class: Brown, Lee, Braggs, and Thomas. (middle top) Worshipful Master, New Hope Lodge No. 3. I would be followed by another son of Wilmington, NC, Edward Whitehead. (middle bottom) I cherished witnessing Worshipful Master Willie Clark Jr. ascend to the East. He was the first Master Mason I brought through to assend to the East. (bottom) I was honored to charter Doris Miller Lodge No 6. On December 7, 2018.

Brother Alphonso Braggs
Alpha Phi Alpha Fraternity, Inc.
Mu Beta Lambda Chapter
Line Number: 1
Name: Atomic Ace
Line Name: 2 Reflections of One
Crossed: November 13, 2010, 9:39 pm, Honolulu, Hawaii
Chapter President – 2020
Life Member No 14844

(top) Celebrating with my chapter brothers on the evening I became an Alpha man at the home of Bro William Griffin. (middle) I was given the honor of serving as Scholarship Committee Chair. Our winners posed with Admiral Cecil Haney, the guest speaker for our annual Black and Gold Ball. (bottom) The brothers are fully committed to developing our future. Our "Alpha Stars" mentoring program had us out early in the morning volunteering at a Boy Scouts service project.

(above) My Alpha line brother, the "Honorable" James Brown.
(below) Celebrating with the chapter brothers at our annual founders day event.

www.ingramcontent.com/pod-product-compliance
Lightning Source LLC
Chambersburg PA
CBHW081155290426
44108CB00018B/2565